What people are saying about "Outcast to Outstanding" and the author

"I reviewed the book and presented the book material to our group of physicians who found it extremely helpful in order to properly identify and properly help these patients in our practice. None of us felt we had a good background in this topic and this book was a *hugely* important instrument and tool in helping us better identify and help these kids." **Dr. Michael J. Milobsky, MD, Pediatrician**

"I devoured this book ... it gives the appropriate tools to empower a parent that they can in fact change and control behaviors to help their child be successful. As a speech pathologist and parent of a child with sensitive divergent needs, I am very excited to share this with colleagues, family members, and families I work with. For a professional it is full of strategies to use in your sessions and shared with and taught to the parents or caregiver of the child you are treating. I remember the expectation of coming into Luiza's home and being the professional wanting to unload all of my well educated knowledge, and instead leaving with notes and strategies from Luiza that I wanted to use in my own home. Luiza is obviously a Mom dealing with these difficulties every day." **Sara Schwesinger - MS, CCC-SLP (speech-language pathology); parent of 2**

"I found myself laughing a few times, nodding multiple times and I appreciated your writing as interesting, real life and engaging." **Karen Pinsky - Board Certified Behavior Analyst® (BCBA)**

"This book is an excellent resource ... I thought the analogy of a person with Sensory Processing Disorder was excellent as SPD is sometimes difficult to explain to parents. I liked the overview of characteristics of SPD and the suggested strategies were right on. Information on other techniques such as social stories, behavioral strategies, visual schedules, transitioning, and token system are very helpful too. Luiza's own behavioral techniques were great and plan to use them on my 6 year old grandson who has ADHD." **Pamela Campos, Registered Occupational Therapist (OTR)**

Luiza's experience raising children with asynchronous developmental patterns has allowed her to provide expert guidance on a path that allows children an optimal level of success. She is an innovator in the field of gifted education. By following the path she outlines in her book, Luiza has been able to maximize the potential of her highly gifted children. **Christopher P. Neville, Principal, Soaring Hawk Elementary**

"There is a lot of wonderful information in this book that are very helpful to many parents that I work with, and to anyone who work with children." **Joy Jensen - Educational Assistant to SED (Severely Emotionally Disabled) Students**

"This book is written from the heart. It tells of the author's personal fight to gain acceptance for her son with special needs in a world that shows compassion and acceptance for the physically challenged but negative labeling and exclusion for the neurologically/behaviorally challenged. The author shares what has worked and not worked on her journey of integrating her son into a world that sometimes doesn't understand, to help others on a similar journey." **Jane McConnell, Early Childhood Educator; mother of 2**

"I highly recommend this book for anyone caring for kids. It provides great insight, personal stories, intriguing visuals, and proven strategies to help give parents, caretakers and teachers the tools to help you best care for a child who may have extra challenges, but is just as important in this world. I also LOVED your vulnerability. I'm not gonna lie, I got choked up." **Ernest Smith - Lead Pastor, Front Range Christian Church; father of 2**

"The book gives you a great view from the child's eyes and helps parents understand what the child needs to be successful." **Mike Giorgio - Behavioral Therapist**

"You're very raw, authentic and genuine and it shows your heart and how you ache for other families to grow also so they can be successful in diagnosing, loving and learning how to function with special needs children … I only wish my parents had a guide like this back in the day … it really opened my eyes and helped me to understand the symptoms, why they are reacting the way they are and what happens if the issues are not addressed." **Lydia Savino - Mother of 10 and 13 year old boys**

"Luiza is amazing at understanding the problem and empathizing with both the parent's and the child's struggles, and explaining methods that will overcome the issues. Luiza's ideas to help with my 17 year old son are amazing and very smart". **Heidi Behren- CPA, mother of 22, 17, 13 year old**

"I am thrilled about this book which will help so many families. I love the book and can't wait to buy copies and hand them out! ... Personal anecdotes help people feel like they aren't alone, increase empathy and provide a visual component in readers' minds." **Mary Anne Scott, mother of 9 & 7 year old boys**

"I found Outcast to Outstanding very enlightening. It was easy to read and understand. I especially liked learning about how to create structure into my children's lives, being consistent in routines and setting up a weekly schedule and even a daily schedule was very beneficial to me and my family. Even if you do not have a sensitive Divergent needs child, this book have different strategies and ideas on how to make your home and lives more smoothly. **Amy Wolfe, mother of 2**

"Your strategies speak to all, Sensitive Divergent Needs child or not, and would be beneficial for any parent/caregiver/teacher to read to deal with all situations that may arise during the growth of any child. I really enjoyed reading your book and have learned some practical techniques to use on my own children." **Erin Dohrman, mother of 3**

Outcast to Outstanding

Outcast to Outstanding

**THE PRACTICAL GUIDE TO UNDERSTANDING
& ADDRESSING THE DRIVERS OF
YOUR CHILD'S BEHAVIOR**

Luiza Y. Coscia

Outcast to Outstanding
The practical guide to understanding & addressing the drivers of your child's behavior

© 2017 Harmonious Clan
All rights reserved. No portion of this book may be reproduced, stored in a retrieval system, or transmitted in any form or by any means – electronic, mechanical, photocopy, recording, scanning, or other – except for brief quotations in critical reviews or articles, without the prior written permission of the publisher.

Design and Illustrations by: Marco A. Coscia

ISBN: 0692925651
ISBN 13: 9780692925652

Dedication

*To my late father –
an extraordinary man
who achieved far more than expected*

Table of Contents

Dedication · ix

What Is Outcast To Outstanding · · · · · · · · · · · ·xv

Is this book for you? · xix

Disclaimer · xxi

Forward · xxiii

Acknowledgements ·xxvii

Introduction · xxix

Section I - Understanding the Child with Sensitive Divergent Needs (SDN) – Cultivating the Soil · · · · · · · · · · · · · · · · · · · 1
Chapter 1   Illusion or Reality? · · · · · · · · · · · 3

	Chapter 2	The Child's Perspective · · · · · · 10
	Chapter 3	What's Really Happening? · · · · 22

Section II - Success Paradigm: Sowing the Seeds · · · · 43
	Chapter 4	The Game Plan That Fuels Outstanding Behaviors · · · · · · · 45
	Chapter 5	The Energy Shift That Transforms the Failure Cycle to the Success Cycle · · · · · · · · 60
	Chapter 6	The Language that Elates & Elevates Your Child · · · · · · · · · · 67

Section III - Meeting Internal Needs: Tending the Seedlings · 75
	Chapter 7	The Surprising Actions That Dramatically Influence and Improve Behaviors · · · · · · · · · · 77
	Chapter 8	The Framework That Deflates Your Child's Anxiety · · · · · · · · 103
	Chapter 9	The Simple Amazing Tool That Boosts Your Child's Cooperation · · · · · · · · · · · · · · 110

Chapter 10	The 7 Effective Techniques That Achieve Successful Transitions ················ 117
Chapter 11	The Powerful, Easy to Implement Process That Simplifies the Teaching of New Behaviors ············· 125

Section IV - Transforming External Behaviors: Reaping the Fruit ···················· 137

Chapter 12	The 3 Letters that Demystify Behaviors ················· 139
Chapter 13	The Remedy for Unplugging Power Struggles············ 149
Chapter 14	The Ultimate System to Ignite a Child's Self-Motivation······ 156
Chapter 15	The Single Action That Stops Behaviors in Their Tracks ····· 165
Chapter 16	The Powerful Dialog That Beckons a Child's Inner Goodness················· 175
Chapter 17	Encouragement ············ 184

Afterword: Taking the first step · · · · · · · · · · 187

Appendix: Selecting the right
professionals · 191

Six ways to put Outcast to Outstanding
to work for you· 199

About the author · 203

What Is Outcast To Outstanding

> "Rough diamonds may sometimes
> be mistaken as ... pebbles"
> – Thomas Browne

Behavior struggles in a brilliant child are like the rough outer surface of an unpolished diamond that obscures the inner gem. A child with behavior challenges can be mistaken as a "problem", an outcast. Only when we polish away the roughness on the surface of the rock, can the internal beauty shine through, revealing the gem. When you polish off your child's behavioral challenges, can you imagine the beautiful gem the world will see? How would that change your child's life?

If only we can polish away that outer roughness (behavioral challenges) for a child.

The problem is, behaviors are only the tip of the iceberg - you can't truly fix the behaviors until you address all the underlying causes beneath the waterline.

Outcast to Outstanding reveals the underlying causes beneath the waterline and explains step-by-step exactly how to address them, *so you can effectively get to the tip of the iceberg and make lasting behavioral transformation.*

What Is Outcast to Outstanding?

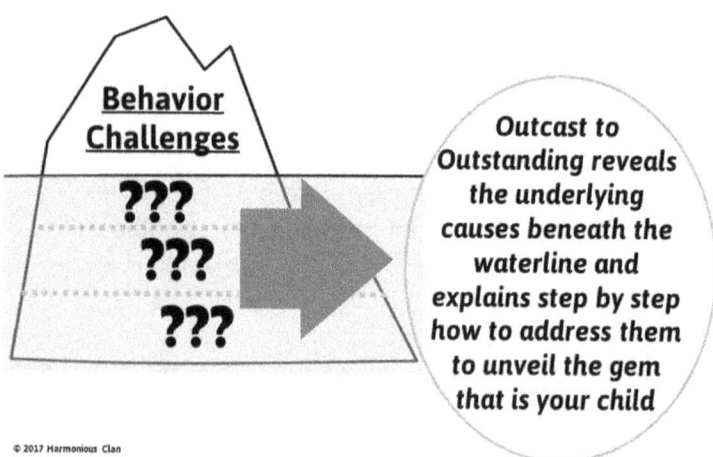

© 2017 Harmonious Clan

Outcast to Outstanding brings to the table **a fresh perspective on how we intervene behaviors – it's not just a matter of discipline** and treating behaviors; but rather, **it's about understanding the child's internal environment and addressing the missing pieces in the internal environment that surface as behaviors**. Most people treat the behavioral symptoms instead of the cause. If we are only looking at the behaviors, we are missing the mark.

Outcast to Outstanding
- helps you understand the drivers of your child's behavior
- shows you how to address the underlying causes of behaviors
- gives you the key to lasting behavior transformation

If you research enough, read enough, work enough with professionals, if you try and fail enough times, you may figure it out on your own. But how many more summers and vacations do you want to spend being frustrated with your child's behavior or trying to figure this all out? Time is going by and your child is growing up. The time you lose will never come back. I went through years of research, working with professionals, trials and errors, tears and pain, and I put this information together here for you so that you don't have to pay the price I paid. This book cuts to the chase and <u>saves you the time, physical and emotional energy, and money spent trying to figure this all out on your own while your child is growing up</u>. The sooner you polish off the rough surface and get to the diamond, the sooner you get to enjoy your child and create lifelong memories.

Remember, inside the outer rough surface is the fine gemstone that is your real child. Once polished, all of your child's talents, genius, and beauty will finally shine through. This book will guide you through the process.

Is this book for you?

If you are a parent, caregiver, teacher/educator, pediatric physician/therapist/professional, or anyone who cares for or works with children, this book is written for you.

If your child or the children you work with have *any* of the following characteristics, this book is a must-read for you:

- Strong-willed
- "Difficult"
- Behaviorally challenged
- Disorganized/scattered-minded
- Gifted (gifted, highly gifted, exceptionally gifted, profoundly gifted)
- ADHD
- Sensory Processing Disorder
- Autism or Asperger's
- Learning disabilities or difficulties
- Anxiety

- Bipolar
- Oppositional Defiant

What you will gain from this book:

- Simple but powerful strategies to improve your child's behavior (that will also enhance your relationship with your child)
- Understanding of your child's internal needs
- Step-by-step guidance to support your child's internal needs
- Knowledge to address the underlying causes of behaviors
- Confidence and empowerment in your parenting
- Relief from your current struggles with your child
- Key to lasting behavior transformation.

Disclaimer

I put this content together based on my experience through a lot of research, book reading, working with numerous professionals, sorting out what works by experimenting over the years, and working in the trenches. Through all this I built these strategies. This is <u>not to be considered as medical advice</u>; but rather, practical strategies to help you and your child's life go **from chaos to harmony, from outcast to outstanding**.

If your child needs medical care, please consult with the appropriate professionals listed in the back of the book (titled "Resources: The right professionals")

Forward

I met Luiza Coscia and her five children in their home where Luiza was home schooling 4 children with a baby in her arms. As we moved through Luiza's home, the reasons why and how her children were so successful despite their challenges were all around us. The way Luiza spoke to the children and the children's predictable schedule and routine was evident as the children knew what to do, but simply checked in to be sure they were on the right track. Luiza had visuals mapping out behavioral sequence expectations (i.e. washing hands sequence on the bathroom mirror) all around the house. Dust pans were arranged on hooks at the smallest children's eye levels so they could reach them and help clean up. Luiza clearly knew how to use her words to communicate with children and how to arrange the environment in ways that promote independence in young children's repertoires resulting in a home with 5 children that was run like a well-oiled machine.

I have been trained as a special education teacher and also as a behavior analyst. I have worked with people with special needs for 25 years in homes, schools, and in the community. I specialize in teaching kids with autism and also have experience working with children with learning disabilities, anxiety disorders, severe behavior challenges, and what some folks refer to as "sensory" challenges. Anyone who has worked with kids for any period of time knows pretty quickly that consideration of what behavior analysts' call "setting events" must not be ignored for a successful intervention.

Setting events can help us understand why people respond to the same situations in different ways. For example, a child who has had a good night sleep and has eaten a solid breakfast on Monday morning will have a successful morning at school. This child quickly and accurately completes all response requirements made by the teacher all morning. The next day, the same child had a rough night sleeping and woke up too late to have breakfast. That Tuesday, the morning is chaotic. This child is unable to follow any of the teacher's expectations and struggles to get through her day. The teacher is puzzled. How can the same child be so different from Monday to Tuesday? The answer will likely lie in the hunger and tiredness this child experiences, as those states have clearly altered the child's ability to perform. It becomes so difficult to meet the classroom expectations under those conditions that the child is completely unsuccessful. Working toward understanding setting events that impact a child's responding is imperative when teaching and Luiza does an outstanding job in helping us all see the child's behavior more clearly.

Chapter 2 is a MUST read for every single person who is attempting to teach a child! When I was starting out teaching in ABA programs for young children with autism, I recall a young client who was unable to allow her hair to be brushed. The adults around her simply believed she was "misbehaving" and she should just be able to sit still and get her hair brushed. Then, I read Temple Grandin's words explaining that getting her hair brushed as a child felt like sandpaper being rubbed across her head. No reinforcers on this planet, no matter how strong would get a person through that type of experience. Until we can even attempt to see through the eyes of the children we are trying to teach, we will fall flat. We can never know for sure, but by trying to understand the child's view, we will be much more effective – and as it turns out – more caring and compassionate – as we choose evidenced based interventions informed by an analysis of the individual child's needs, including those needs that we cannot see with our eyes, but the child's behavior provides cues.

This book, "Outcast to Outstanding" describes useful and helpful strategies to deal with children that Luiza describes as having "Sensitive Divergent Needs". These children are likely highly sensitive to environmental stimulation such as too many people, temperature changes, noise, or various textures resulting in inabilities to regulate, manifesting as behavioral challenges. These children may be very bright and have the ability to, for example, learn complex math by the time they are 5 years old, but still struggle mysteriously at times to meet the demands in various environments due to noise, too many people, temperature changes, or have the need to physically move much more than their same aged peers. When setting events are related to inabilities to sit still, inabilities to regulate emotions, or inabilities to focus and listen – there are ways to support children so they have the opportunity to be more successful and get closer to reaching their maximum potential. By attempting to understand the child's point of view regarding what a particular child is experiencing, it can inform our interventions addressing the observed behaviors we treat. This book does just that and will prove an extremely valuable tool.

It is important to state that the daily success Luiza has with her children is directly related to the amount of research, guidance, processing and understanding of the research, and environmental arrangement she has put in to help her children reach their maximum potential. Luiza makes it look easy. It is not. It took dedication to evidence based strategies in researching, trying and adjusting on Luiza's part until she found the correct routines and systems, continuously tweaking systems along the way. The strategies Luiza has implemented, making it all look so easy, are all presented in this book.

Good luck and have fun!!!
Karen Pinsky, Board Certified Behavior Analyst

Acknowledgements

To my parents for raising me with the values of hard work and perseverance; for doing their best with everything they had, and for always giving their very best.

To my husband, Marco, for editing and illustrating the book; for being my best friend, business partner, and life partner; for encouraging and helping me realize my aspirations; for your talents and creativity, your love, and the life we share together.

To my five children (so far) for laughter, joy and tears; for placing a continuous string of challenges on me without ever letting me off the hook; for the pulling-my-hair-out days, and for the most gratifying non-paid job in the world.

To my behavior expert, Karen Pinsky, for supporting me and confirming that my ideas are consistent with her theoretical studies and decades of industry experience; for her dedication to children with differentiating needs.

To my mentor, Charles Philippe, for believing in me, stretching me, and being there for me.

To my cheerleader and special need professional, Sara Schwesinger, for your endorsement and your professional insights; for your generous spirit of support in my work and my own parenting.

To my Sensory Processing guru, Pamela Campos, for your professional and technical validation; for your keenness that encouraged me; for your compassion for children.

To all who read and reviewed the book for me, thank you for your enthusiasm and support.

Thank you to all of you.

Introduction

As depicted in the figure below, behaviors are just the tip of the iceberg. You can see from the figure that there is a lot more lurking below the visible tip of the iceberg. In order to address challenging and maladaptive behaviors, you must address the layers beneath the iceberg. This book teaches you how to do that step by step and the sections are noted for reference.

Sensitive Divergent Needs (SDN)

In this book, I define the term a child with 'Sensitive Divergent Needs' (SDN) as a child that has an acute sensitivity with a lack of regulation and divergent physiological, mental, and emotional needs that result in challenging behavioral problems and difficulties in daily life. This book is written to help you support and nurture the child with SDN.

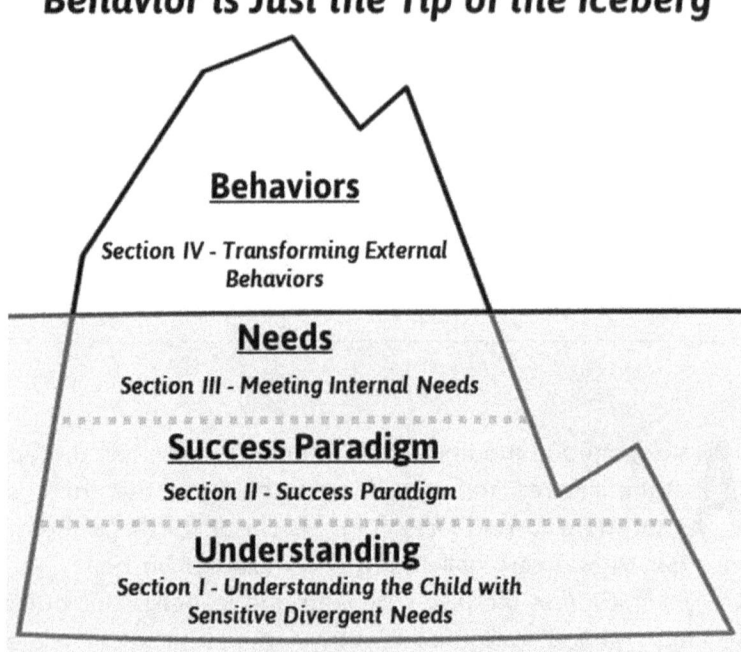

Figure 1 Behavior is Just the Tip of the Iceberg

From Chaos to Harmony

The nature of caring for a child with SDN can put your life on a chaotic path. This book is written to equip you with practical strategies that you can use daily to organize your child's internal system and external behaviors from chaos to harmony.

From Outcast to Outstanding

The 4 major steps to nurture your child from outcast to outstanding are organized into 4 sections in this book:

I. Understanding the child with Sensitive Divergent Needs (SDN) – Cultivating the Soil

In order to address the challenging behaviors, we must first understand the factors that impact the daily life of a child with SDN. Chapters 1-3 will open your eyes to their struggles and explain their behaviors.

II. Success Paradigm – Sowing the Seed

Next, we need to give the child a Success Paradigm, which is a reprogram of the child's experience from one of failure to one of success. This ignites and fuels the child to be outstanding. A lot of challenging behaviors will diminished at this step. Chapters 4-6 teach you strategies on how to create this critical paradigm shift.

III. Meeting Internal Needs – Tending the Seedlings

Next, we meet the divergent needs of the child, and more maladaptive behaviors will transform without really addressing behaviors. What are the needs, and how do we meet them? Chapters 7-11 walk you through these practical strategies step by step.

IV. Transforming External Behaviors – Reaping the Fruit

The platform where the divergent needs are properly met and the child has a Success Paradigm allows you to effectively tackle challenging behaviors head on. Chapters 12-16 give you the tools you will need to address behaviors effectively.

Will These Strategies Also Work Well with children who do <u>not</u> have Sensitive Divergent Needs (SDN)?

These strategies not only work well for children with SDN, but also will work extremely well, and even better, for children without SDN. Children with SDN struggle more with behavior challenges due to their various skill deficits that cause internal chaos manifested as external behaviors. You can think of the skill deficits and challenging behaviors on a scale with the various skill deficits and behaviors of children with SDN at the high end of a scale and the children without SDN at the low end of the scale. Most children fall somewhere between those two extremes of the scale. These strategies will work as effectively, or even more effectively, with children <u>without</u> SDN, since they have fewer deficits so you can get to the tip of the iceberg more quickly. The figure below illustrates this concept.

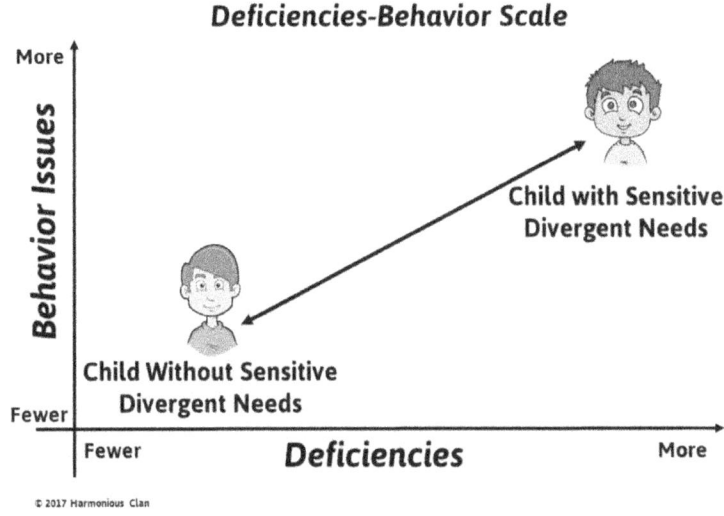

Figure 2 Deficiencies-Behavior Scale Illustration

From Outcast to Outstanding

Children with SDN can be held back by their skill deficits. Many don't have appropriate and sufficient support for their divergent needs, nor do they have people in their lives who will hold up the high expectations on them despite their deficiencies, pushing them to achieve their maximum developmental potential. My philosophy is to **provide the appropriate support for their deficiencies while nurturing their potential - bridge the gap on the lower end while pushing the ceiling on the higher end**.

Section I - Understanding the Child with Sensitive Divergent Needs (SDN) - Cultivating the Soil

CHAPTER 1
Illusion or Reality?

♦ ♦ ♦ ♦ ♦ ♦ ♦ ♦ ♦ ♦ ♦ ♦ ♦ ♦ ♦ ♦ ♦

What You Will Learn In This Chapter:

✓ What a child with Sensitive Divergent Needs (SDN) looks like from the outside
✓ See an example of a typical social situation that the child with SDN may experience
✓ Get a better understanding of how the outsiders view the child with SDN

♦ ♦ ♦ ♦ ♦ ♦ ♦ ♦ ♦ ♦ ♦ ♦ ♦ ♦ ♦ ♦ ♦

A child with Sensitive Divergent Needs (SDN) is a child who has an acute sensitivity with a lack of regulation, and divergent physiological, mental, and emotional needs that result in challenging behavioral problems and difficulties in daily life.

In order to understand the child with SDN, it is best to look at the child from the view of the observer in a real life situation. The following story will help illustrate how the world may view a child with SDN. The observer sees only the outward facing behaviors and responses of the child with SDN without knowledge of what is going on inside the child that is creating the outward symptoms. I call this 'the outsiders view', or the casual observer (parents, other children, teachers, camp leaders, etc.) viewpoint.

Chapter 3 through the end of the book **teach you practical strategies to nurture your child from outcast to outstanding.** Outcast to outstanding in this context means **taking the children who are socially outcast because of their externally exhibited behavior problems caused by their Sensitive Divergent Needs, and bringing them to the place of outstanding. Their behaviors transform to outstanding when you properly address their Sensitive Divergent Needs (SDN).**

Picture this scene.

A five year old boy ("The Theater Child") walks into his first day of his first theater camp. He is impeccably dressed with his best shirt, pants and hat that he picked out himself. The child also has earplugs in his ears. His excitement about this camp has been building for weeks, ever since his parents offered him the option to attend. He walks into the room and he finds a seat in the front row center and eagerly waits for what's going to happen here.

More children begin to filter into the room. Another boy walks to the front and takes a seat right next to The Theater Child. The boy turns towards The Theater Child and makes his silly faces, acts his silly way - a rather fashionable greeting from an over-energized young boy. The Theater Child turns away without saying anything, and he returns his attention back to the stage, waiting for that adult (teacher) to show up to start the camp. At this time, The Theater Child's mother gives him a good-bye hug and wishes him a good day. The mother also gave a heads-up to the camp teacher and director about the Theater Child's special needs, hoping that the staff would be able to support the child better, knowing the background. The camp teacher reassured the mother that she was a special needs teacher with special education background, and not to worry at all.

Just before noon, the mother receives a call from the theater director stating that The Theater Child is crying, screaming and yelling uncontrollably for no apparent reason. They reported that the child is now sitting at the theater's director's office screaming and yelling and he would not tell them why he is upset. The camp teachers cannot fathom why The Theater Child would, out of the blue, start screaming, yelling and throwing an out of control tantrum. To the teachers, this child caused a commotion and then had a tantrum and had to be taken to the office. The Theater Child's mother is not sure how to respond to what appears to be a random acting out by her son.

Fortunately, The Theater Child's therapist is scheduled to come to the theater (to accompany/support/help the child) right about this time. The therapist walks into the middle of this crazy nonsensical screaming, yelling, and crying. She has no idea what could have set him off, and neither do the camp's teachers tell her anything about what happened. The staff indicated that there wasn't anything that set The Theater Child off. They indicated that he randomly started all this craziness and that he is in his own world. They explained that no one was able to calm him down or get him to stop his screaming and that he was not responding to anyone.

The therapist sent numerous text messages to The Theater Child's mother asking what can possibly calm down this child, but nothing worked. The theater child went on with his crazy outburst and did not recover for at least two hours. For two hours he was in no condition to be brought back to the theater room where all the other children were having fun and enjoying their theater camp. When he finally was stabilized enough from his episode to be brought back to the room, he refused to do anything – he would not get on stage, he would not say a line, he would not look at people, he would not respond to anything that the teacher asked. He appeared nothing but odd and scary to the teachers and other camp students.

At the end of day 1 when the mother picked up the Theater Child, the mother tried to talk with the camp teacher (the special education teacher) trying to understand what happened with her son that day. The teacher interrupted the mother's request to talk and said "I don't know anything about it", and dismissed the mother. The teacher seemed to not want to discuss anything, to the degree of cutting the mother off and sending the mother away. Perhaps she knew that her actions had escalated the situation and felt self-conscious?

As the week-long theater camp went on, each day there was another report about The Theater Child. On day two when the mother picked him up, the camp teacher reported that he had punched another child in the stomach very hard, at the doughnut shop where the camp kids went for snack that day, TOTALLY OUT OF THE BLUE! "Nobody was bothering him and he just came right up and punched that boy to the floor!" Everyone thought this child was crazy and random. It was clear at this point to the Theater Childs mom that the Theater Child had been labeled as the problem child, the bully, the one who disrupts what would otherwise be a peaceful and fun camp.

The Theater Child spent camp Day 3 and Day 4 with his other therapist accompanying him. There was no outrageous behavior report, but he never said his lines; he didn't get on stage very much. He did not participate in any games or any camp activities. He did not do much of anything while at the camp those two days.

Day 5 was the last day of camp, and it was show day, the day when the camp students put on a show for all the parents and teachers showcasing the performance they had worked so hard to put together the whole week of camp. The Theater Child was not in the performance. And what could you expect after all of The Theater Child's craziness and inability to do anything that was required at the camp. On the performance day, based on his performance in the last four days, he had no part, no line, and no spot on the stage. To the teachers it was a relief that The Theater Child was not in the show. He would not be causing any embarrassment during the performance or mess up anything for the production on such a big day.

The Theater Child, with his mother's support on Day 5, did get up on that stage. What the Theater Child had expected to be a fun camp and a chance to showcase his imagination and performance skills had turned horribly wrong. He went up on stage without a real line to perform and without the other children allowing a real space for him to be on stage. He did his best, but looked broken and beaten down. He had been a victim of a worldview that sees only the outwards signs, symptoms and actions of a 'problem' child. Nobody cared or knew enough about what was really going on to take that child, understand him and include him in the camp's activities. Instead, he was cast aside like damaged goods and excluded from the very activity that he so loved, acting and performing, using his imagination to be something beyond himself.

It's no wonder many children like the Theater Child end up turning inward, focusing on their own world with little self-esteem. The Theater Child feels like a failure and feels he cannot do what other children do. His self-esteem is crushed and he begins to doubt himself even more. He begins to lose interest in his imaginary play and his desire to perform. The theater Child's dreams now seem unreachable.

A first step in understanding and helping children like the Theater Child is to turn the focus from the camera view to the child's view. For only after understanding the scenario from the child's view (in Chapter 2), does one have the perspective, empathy and strategies to assist the child. When one understands the child's perspective and understands what is going on inside the child, can one begin to be more inclusive with the child and allow this child the opportunity to participate in and enjoy in the activities of childhood. Chapter 2 will take look at The Theater Child's perspective to help in that understanding.

◆ ◆ ◆ ◆ ◆ ◆ ◆ ◆ ◆ ◆ ◆ ◆ ◆ ◆ ◆ ◆

Your Take-away from this chapter:

- ✓ Understanding how social situations and social dynamics can amplify behavior issues in children with SDN
- ✓ Without proper strategies and support, the behavior of a child with SDN can quickly get out of control, becoming a social outcast

◆ ◆ ◆ ◆ ◆ ◆ ◆ ◆ ◆ ◆ ◆ ◆ ◆ ◆ ◆ ◆

CHAPTER 2
The Child's Perspective

◆ ◆ ◆ ◆ ◆ ◆ ◆ ◆ ◆ ◆ ◆ ◆ ◆ ◆ ◆ ◆

What You Will Learn In This Chapter:

- ✓ What's causing the challenging behaviors
- ✓ What it feels like to the child with Sensitive Divergent Needs (SDN)

◆ ◆ ◆ ◆ ◆ ◆ ◆ ◆ ◆ ◆ ◆ ◆ ◆ ◆ ◆ ◆

In Chapter 1, you saw The Theater Child from the camera view - precisely how he looks to an outsider, and precisely how the world views him. Everyone has seen one of these children before. There is one in almost every class you walk into - the child who causes a lot of trouble or who is the misfit. You are mistaken if you think that is really the child. Sadly, that child, as captured on camera by the world's view, is not at all the real child. The child and the behavior the world saw was a result of him being in an environment that doesn't support his Sensitive Divergent Needs (SDN).

For a moment, let's turn off the camera and let's view the story from The Theater Child's perspective. Here is what was really going on from the child's view:

Days before The Theater Child's very first theater camp, he had begged and reminded his busy parents over and over to wash his hat for him, "so it would look clean and perfect for my theater camp". Performing, acting, playing someone else is right up his alley. It's what he lives to do, every day, morning to night. One moment he is King Arthur, then he is one of the Knights of the Round Table, swinging his sword saying 'Thoust must be brave as we fight for our liberty against the evil that is invading our kingdom... CHARGE' with his Old English accent. The next moment he has a stuffed animal lion in one hand, an ugly puppet creature in another, and he is acting out Chronicles of Narnia which he read. In a deep strong voice saying, "Aslan's death is coming tonight. It is the battle of good and evil. When the time comes, Aslan's son shall be the king....." In his world, **he can be anyone, anything, and everything**. He is full of personality and talent, and the sky is the limit.

The anticipation of an event as fantastic as theater camp overflows in him. The morning of camp's first day, he walked out of his bedroom dressed up in button down shirt tucked into his well-coordinated pants with a leather belt around his waist and his finally-washed-clean "lucky" hat over his head. So happily he asked, "Mama! Do I look dashing today?" He really cares about this camp. "This is going to be nothing but awesome!" he thought to himself.

The Theater Child walks into the first day of his first theater camp and he doesn't know what to expect. As he walks into the theater, his heart is pounding with a great deal of excitement and anticipation. He finds the front row in the center and takes a seat there, eagerly awaiting what's going to happen on the stage; anticipating what the teacher will do.

Although he is already wearing ear plugs in his ears, the sound of people talking, the AC running, the far-away restroom toilet flushing, the echo in the room, all of it, is still very difficult for his impaired <u>auditory processing system</u> – to him it is a SCREECHING high pitched roar in his ears! As more and more children walk into the room, the lights, the pattern of lined seats, the movements of kids passing around him, the blinds, the patterns of the carpet, the wall pictures, the contrast with the white wall, the texture of the walls and ceiling are all stabbing into his compromised <u>visual processing system</u>. The texture of the seat he is in is beginning to aggravate his inadequate <u>tactile system</u>. Within 30 seconds, his entire neurological and sensory system is in overload and under attack from his environment.

He had been thinking about this camp for weeks. He has been anticipating having a chance to get up on stage and do what he loves, to act and use his imagination. But now he just wants to scream; he wants to get up and run away from it all and relieve his system from the forceful multi-directional charge because he is under a sensory attack. Yet he doesn't want to fail at this important camp, so he continues to sit in his seat with the war going on inside of his body, waiting for the camp teacher to start the action. Meanwhile, while in this already heightened state, another boy walks up to The Theater Child, takes a seat next to him and starts making silly faces and sounds and waving his hands all over in The Theater Child's face (just a fashionable greeting). The Theater Child experiences this as another point of sensory charge, a visual and auditory alarm to his immature neurological system. To the Theater Child the other child's actions are a RED light, a personal space invasion and a multi-sensory attack on his system. The Theater Child looks as if he is seated calmly, but internally he is at war. He is thinking to himself "I must remain still to be here", "I am not going to fail at this". The Theater Child once again tries to battle his distressed sensory system as he manages to turn away from the distraction of the boy next to him and tune himself back to the stage, where the teacher is now standing.

The Theater Child's brain is seeking *proprioceptive input* to orient itself with situational awareness data, which all our brains constantly do, except his brain never receives the data due to disconnected neurons. This lack of input is making it increasingly harder for him to keep himself together. The Theater Child tries his best to survive the **continuous** sensory overload and to attend to the teacher while keeping himself together. But more stimulation is coming when suddenly the boy next to him smacks The Theater Child in his face with his 3-ring binder. To The Theater Child someone dropped an explosive bomb on him and The Theater Child now really has no option but to externally defend himself and his sensory system by smacking the other child right back. The teacher calls out The Theater Child and asks him to leave the theater room immediately. The Theater Child is thinking "me, I didn't do anything wrong except try my best to leave the boy alone numerous times while fighting my internal battle, and I ONLY acted out to defend myself when <u>absolutely necessary</u>". The Theater Child looks down, speechless and hopeless knowing he has probably now lost his opportunity to participate in the camp that he has so anticipated these many weeks. He is speechless, as he is truly unable to speak for himself due to a distressed sensory system and a developmental neurological disorder. The Theater Child's conditions make just about everything in his life a hundred times harder than it is, including opening his mouth to talk at this very moment. Hopeless, because he well knows that without the ability to speak, to assert himself and to self-advocate when wronged, he is truly hopeless and doomed to be a silent victim of unjust treatment. At the same time, he is confused, "why am *I* the one being kicked out of the theater when I have been working so hard to be here?"

The Theater Child's impaired sensory system never stopped being attacked. You may think the biggest bomb had already dropped on this poor child, but there is more to come. Here come fifty jets firing missiles at him -- the teacher walks up to The Theater Child, pulls his hands and body out of his seat, which sets off a FLASHING RED LIGHT to The Theater Child as a MAJOR sensory attack hits him - somebody is unexpectedly touching his body! The camp teacher takes him all the way out of the room, because enough is enough since a person can only take so much of this unruly behavior. To the Theater Child this has been distressing and offensive, both at a <u>sensory</u>

OUTCAST TO OUTSTANDING

<u>level</u> and <u>personal level</u>, from the minute he walked in the door to the theater camp, through all the sensory overload, to the smack in the face, to the last straw of being pulled out of the room in front of the whole class. Now the problem has taken a turn from sensory to sensory plus humiliation. He has no words to speak out against his unjust and humiliating treatment. Even if he did, no one would have believed him given that HE was the one who was called out and removed by the teacher, not the boy who initiated the offense. No words can wash him clean and give him his dignity back. The only thing left for The Theater Child was tears and painful screams as loud and for as long as it takes for him to get all the wrong and unjust off his chest and out of his system.

At noon, The Theater Child's therapist walks into the scene. No one at camp would tell her what happened or what was wrong so she can help The Theater Child. **It is much easier to believe and to portray a story that blames <u>the child "with problems"</u> than it is to help nurture and support a child with disability, <u>a child with "differences"</u>, differences that are "wonderfully and fearfully made"**.

From noon through the rest of the afternoon, the therapist cannot figure out what is going on, and neither could The Theater Child speak about it. He could only cry about it. The Theater Child knew that he was beginning to form a reputation as the inconsolable, out-of-control, "crazy" child. He couldn't help it; he was in too deep of a hole to explain himself. After all, who would understand even how the running AC sound, which most people don't even notice, can sound like a high screech in his ears that literally hurt his ears, let alone the fact that <u>someone other than him</u> could actually be the child who is smacking others? With an overloaded sensory system, it only took him two hours to recompose himself from the event. When he was finally in an "acceptable condition" to walk back into the room, undignified and humiliated, he was in no mental, physical, sensorial, and emotional condition to do anything - including acting a part, saying a line, or getting up on stage. They all say that The Theater Child didn't *want to* perform, but little did they know that they are talking about a surviving soldier who just got carried out of a major bombing and missile attack who *couldn't* perform. Needless to say, he ended up with no part at all for the show while EACH other camp child had three parts.

The Theater Child spent the rest of the camp days feeling smaller and smaller and continuing to fight sensory distress because that is the life of children with neurological disorders and some with sensory difficulties. There continues to be no appropriate support for his challenges, and no repairing action for his self-esteem, only more exclusion and more experiences of failure. This includes a day when he was reported to punch a child in the stomach at the doughnut shop - the same boy who bothered The Theater Child and smacked him in the face on the first day of camp. Is it any surprise the Theater Child acted out against the boy who caused him to go over his sensory edge? People don't see the antecedent events, or precursors that lead to the events. - Having a bunch of kids idly waiting around in a noisy chaotic doughnut shop, which is sensory overload to a child with SDN, while the same boy that caused the overload a day before is now waving his hands, jumping up and down making noises in The Theater Child's face like he did on day one, is an absolute intrusion to his sensory system. People don't see these antecedents, triggers, and sensory difficult interactions. When enough is enough and it comes the moment where The Theater Child punches the other boy, people say it's "TOTALLY OUT OF THE BLUE!", but is it really?

The Theater Child is feeling increasingly more and more undignified and humiliated by his camp experience. Worst of all, as kids push him out of games and try to exclude him from camp activities, the multi-talented, full of personality and enthusiastic Theater Child who once thought he could **be anyone, anything, and everything** is starting to feel ashamed of himself and worthless. There is no rebuild for the loss of self-esteem. Neither can anyone see the tender heart under this "crazy beast" that so desires to be a part of the show and part of the camp experience, but has unjustly been denied the opportunity to do so.

Each night he comes home with a soft voice, "I'm really trying, Mama". "I really would like a part and some lines to perform on stage, just like everybody else at camp, Papa, when will I get to do that?" Since when does The Theater Child not "get to do" the camp activities that all the other camp kids are getting to do?

On the evening of day 4 (the day before the big camp performance show), the helpless mother realizes what's going on - exclusion. Without a childcare option, she takes her three younger children (3 yrs and under) along to the camp to be there the whole day in support of and to advocate for The Theater Child's deep desire just to be a part of an experience that he deserves as equally as the other children. But by day 5 (performance day), The Theater Child's original excitement is all gone and he has pretty much resigned himself to a corner doing nothing but hiding in his drawing pad with his head down drawing the whole morning in a corner of the room.

He is now written out of the show and he is left with no part, no line, and not even a space on the stage for any of the group dances. There was nothing he could do to be in the show even if he wanted to. He wasn't even going to get a costume had his therapist not walked up with him to ask for it. His mother had to fight to get a part for him. During rehearsals, given his therapist's and his mother's support, he was able to perfectly say that one single line his mother fought so hard for him to have. But he had to overcome another child trying to say his line for him. He also felt discouraged as they gave him no space on the stage. While his mother tried fighting for him to have a little bit of space on stage during group dances (he loves music and dances), he literally got pushed off the stage - he FELL OFF THE STAGE into the curtain drip. By now it is somehow established that he doesn't "deserve" a part, a line, or so much as a spot on the stage. The teachers and other children see The Theater Child as the problem that doesn't want to participate and likes to cause havoc. Nothing could be further from the truth. With determination he got back up off the floor and kept trying the hardest he could (yes, while still under sensory overload) to be included in the show, but it just wasn't happening for him.

At show time, he gave it his all. He acted out his only one line with more enthusiasm and personality than any other child, but he still had to stand in the corner of the stage as if he was a loser, staring with no dance partner. He gave it his best and his all to what he was "allowed" to do. But he was not King Arthur, not a knight of the round table, not Aslan in Narnia, not anymore...he was reduced to this small insignificant part in the corner of the stage with no dance partner.

As described in Chapter 1, the camp teacher reassured the mother that she was a special education teacher and for the mother not to worry. The well-intentioned mother didn't know that openly bringing to the teacher's attention the child's special needs could sometimes cause a reason for the child to be treated differently - different in a negative way, not in a positive, supportive way. Instead of calling out the child who instigated The Theater Child, she assumes <u>all problems in the classroom are the result of The Theater Child's problem</u> and therefore she calls him out by default, rather than investigating the facts of what happened. The mother regretted having told the camp teacher that her child had special needs. The mother thought that by revealing this piece of information, all caregivers would extend their warm hands to provide respectful and appropriate support to the conditions of children with special needs. While this may be true in some cases, here, she felt that exposing her son's special needs turned out to be a disadvantage for her son. As a result, the mother thought maybe she should not have considered her son for theater camp no matter how good and passionate he was about acting. She began to feel that taking him anywhere out of the house was a mistake, because it brought judgmental eyes of the world onto her son.

The root of these feelings is based on her experience and her experience was driven by a lack of understanding of the caregiver. Sometimes a lack of understanding causes people to judge instead of reaching out with proper support for the child. This is not always their fault, rather, it exposes the need for awareness, training and skill building on how to handle children with _nonphysical_ special needs.

Awareness brings less judgement and more compassion, which leads to understanding.

Understanding opens the door to the right support.

Chapter 2 Epilog
The Theater Child is my own son.

And the theater camp was not the first or only discouraging experience he had – he had similar experiences everywhere he went.

On day 5 at the theater performance, while every parent proudly watched their children shine on stage in the final performance, I watched the show in tears of sorrow. I was ever so proud of him, yet I was so distraught knowing what he had gone through that week. My heart ached as I watched my **courageous and zestful King Arthur**, who once believed he was undefeatable, now **a dejected soul** no longer trying to squeeze a spot on stage, instead taking his rightful spot all alone in a corner.

The biggest despair for me was to see a child who believed **he could be anything** turned into **a child who thought he was nothing**. Right then and there I decided that no child should experience what my child experienced that night. At that moment, I set foot on my new path, a path to ensure that no child will ever be outcast for his or her divergent needs. I wanted to bring awareness, understanding, and strategies that deliver proper support to our children. That's when I decided to write this book, "*Outcast to Outstanding*".

My husband and I also started Harmonious Clan, whose mission is to equip you with proven practical strategies that give you results, enabling you to nurture your child from outcast to outstanding. We do this by resourcing you with our books, educational podcasts, courses, a supportive community, speaking events and one on one consulting.

Harmonious Clan … <u>enabling you to nurture your child from Outcast to Outstanding</u>

If you have questions, comments, or need additional information or support, please email me directly at luiza@harmoniousclan.com.

♦ ♦ ♦ ♦ ♦ ♦ ♦ ♦ ♦ ♦ ♦ ♦ ♦ ♦ ♦ ♦

Your Take-Away From This Chapter:

- ✓ The behavior is only the tip of the iceberg….
- ✓ Awareness and understanding is necessary to achieve proper support for our children

♦ ♦ ♦ ♦ ♦ ♦ ♦ ♦ ♦ ♦ ♦ ♦ ♦ ♦ ♦ ♦

CHAPTER 3
What's Really Happening?

♦ ♦ ♦ ♦ ♦ ♦ ♦ ♦ ♦ ♦ ♦ ♦ ♦ ♦ ♦

What You Will Learn In This Chapter:

- ✓ What is a child with Sensitive Divergent Needs (SDN)?
- ✓ Why do they act this way? Tour a mile in their shoes and find out
- ✓ Sensory problems vs. Behavioral problems
- ✓ The 'downward spiral' is what happens when the issues aren't addressed

♦ ♦ ♦ ♦ ♦ ♦ ♦ ♦ ♦ ♦ ♦ ♦ ♦ ♦ ♦

In the context of this book, we define a **Child with Sensitive Divergent Needs (SDN)** as a child who has an acute sensitivity to surroundings with a lack of regulation, and divergent physiological, mental, and emotional needs that result in behavioral problems and difficulties in daily life.

SDN is not a particular Diagnostic and Statistical Manual of Mental Disorders (DSM) diagnosis. The purpose of the term SDN is to describe a subset of children who deal with these types of challenges and this book presents strategies to directly address the challenges these children experience. There are many of these children, but not all of them have these issues. This book is geared toward families of children with these specific characteristics.

Typical characteristics of Children with Sensitive Divergent Needs (SDN):

- Easily agitated, frequent meltdowns and tantrums
- Easily overwhelmed/overstimulated - difficulties in crowds, stores, social settings
- Easily distracted, trouble focusing, fidgets
- Behaviorally challenging
- Difficulties switching between tasks and environments
- Rigid & inflexible
- Has quirks - bothered by things that typically don't bother other children, i.e. the way clothing feels on them, food texture, shampoo/showering, etc.
- Acute sensitivity - to surroundings, people, noises, changes, etc.
- Trouble with emotional regulation

Children with SDN may have ADHD, Autism, Sensory Processing Disorder, Bipolar disorder, Anxiety Disorder, Oppositional Defiance Disorder, etc., or any combination of these disorders. The child may also be gifted, highly gifted, or profoundly gifted, or what is known as "twice exceptional (2E)". A twice exceptional child is a child who is gifted, but also has an impairment (a learning disability, developmental disability, or any other diagnoses). We define here the term a child with "Sensitive Divergent Needs (SDN)" to encompass all of the above conditions, as well as many that have <u>no pre-existing formal diagnoses</u> but still struggles. The definition of the term is based on the fact that **children with all or any combination of the above conditions tend to have very similar symptoms. The most common symptom is they all have behavioral challenges resulting from their underlying conditions**. Many of these conditions and diagnoses are also coexisting, making it difficult to separate them.

The illustration below (Figure 3-1) provides an overview of the many different facets of a child with SDN. If your child falls into any of the categories below or seems behaviorally challenged, you may have a child with SDN.

In order for a child with SDN (children with all or some of the above conditions), to be in harmony, not only do we need to meet their needs, but ultimately we want to conquer their behavior challenges. This book presents to you effective strategies that work in meeting the child with SDN's needs and in turning the child's behavior challenges around.

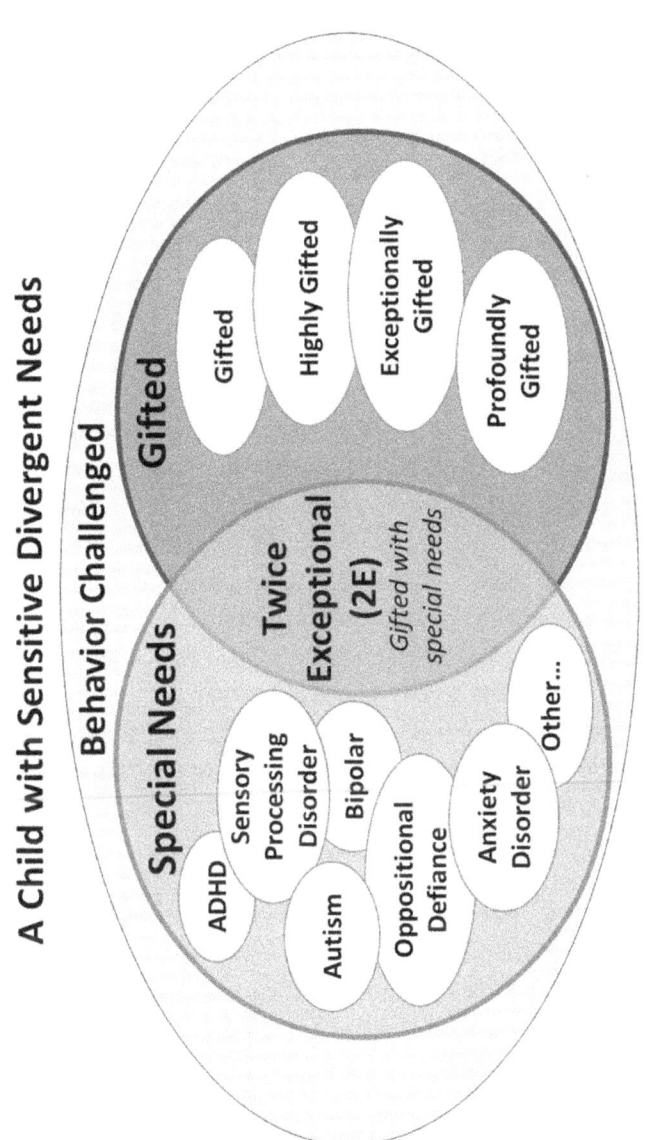

Figure 3- 1 Child with Sensitive Divergent Needs (SDN)

Our Theater Child, as presented in earlier chapters, is a twice exceptional (2E) child who is not only profoundly gifted, but also has multiple complex diagnoses including developmental and learning disabilities. **His profound giftedness masks his disabilities causing him to not receive the proper support for his conditions, and, at the same time, his disabilities and conditions hinder his profound giftedness from flourishing.** The two ends of his "exceptions" (2E) – the gifted end and disabled end, in essence, cancel each other out, and to the world he looks like a child with only behavior problems. People are unable to see and nurture the endless potential of his giftedness since it is masked by his disabilities. Neither can they see his hindering conditions to properly support him because his giftedness masks the disabilities and internal struggles he deals with on a daily basis. In the end, he is treated like "the problem child" who receives neither the nurturing of his capabilities nor the support for his disabilities. He becomes the labeled problem child and is set to chart his own course with a typically non ideal outcome where he fails to achieve at an optimal level. This book addresses these hindering conditions that stand in the way of every child with SDN being the best they can be.

Why do Children with SDN act this way? A mile in their shoes

A typical child with SDN struggles with sensory disintegration, the condition in which the brain is unable to properly receive and respond to information that comes in through the senses.

Let's look at an example of what it is like to walk a mile in the shoes of a child with SDN. Here is a hypothetical analogy to help you understand the world of a child with SDN. Imagine you being sent to the grocery store to get some important items for a party. However, on your drive to the store you realize your windshield is full of dirt, but you can't do anything about it because your wiper doesn't work, so your vision isn't clear. You are covered with ear muffs so big that you can hardly hear any alarming honk from another driver when you unknowingly and unsafely drive into their space and somehow you can't take the earmuffs off. On top of that, your leg is completely numb from your last prolonged sitting, so you can't tell if your foot is actually putting force onto the gas pedal or if your foot is just hanging free. Who knows? You could even be stepping on the brake pedal with full force thinking you are on the gas pedal trying to accelerate for the freeway and not knowing because your whole leg is numb. On top of that, the road has residual snow and with a muddy windshield you really don't know if you're driving on black ice or just a wet spot. You know you need to get to the store and back for the much needed items, but you don't even feel like you can make it to the store safely under these driving conditions. You vaguely hear drivers honking at you left and right, so you suspect you are not where you are supposed to be, but you really can't tell where you are and if they are really honking at you. **You are not blind; you are not deaf; you do have arms and legs, but you just can't orient yourself and can't make your body parts do what they need to do.** As you sit behind the wheel, would you cry? Would you scream out of stress? Would you pull out your best rational under the distress and slam on the break to stop it all, and find the train of cars crashing into you due to your irrational sudden stop? Or better yet, would you try so carefully to pull over somewhere safe, but end up crashing into a pole because you couldn't hit the break when you got to the curb? What could you do behind the wheel?

Really, there is nothing you can do besides waiting for the big crash if you can't get clear information about your orientation and your orientation with respect to your surroundings, despite that your eyes, ears, arms, legs and all body parts work just fine. This is the life of a child with SDN. Their impaired sensory system makes it such that they can see, but still can't orient themselves with their surroundings; they can hear but can't process what they are hearing in order to respond appropriately; they can feel but can't tell whether they are forcing on the gas pedal or not even touching the pedal. It is nearly impossible and frustrating to live like this. Do you see a reason for the meltdowns (like when you were under so much stress behind the wheels)? Do you see a reason for the irrational behaviors (like when you just decided to slam on the break in the middle of the road because you couldn't drive anymore)? Do you see a reason for failures despite the best attempts (like when you drove your car into the pole even though pulling to the curb was the only rational thing to do)?

The child with SDN is far more chaotic and insecure. They are constantly feeling what you're feeling behind the wheel - everything is very SCARY to them. They need far more support to compensate for and eventually grow beyond these factors. Now you look at one of these Children with SDN and wonder, "how do you function like this?" And that's exactly the point - they don't, or not very well at least. This is a mile in their shoes.

Another example is that most people are able to carry on a conversation in a coffee shop by filtering out background noises. A child with SDN may not be able to filter out unimportant information, resulting in system overload, which manifests behaviorally (misbehavior or eventual meltdown). Many challenging behaviors result from the internal system's inability to regulate sensory inputs. Possible impaired sensory areas include: auditory, visual, tactile, olfactory, gustatory, vestibular (movement), and proprioception (body awareness).

Sensory Processing Disorder

In many cases, a big part of the reason that Children with SDN have such a difficult time and so many behavior challenges is due to underlying sensory issues. The sensory issues are defined as Sensory Processing Disorder (SPD), which is also known as Sensory Integration Dysfunction.

Even though sensory processing issues exist in a majority of children and adults on the autism spectrum, they also exist in children with Attention Deficit Hyperactivity Disorder (ADHD), Obsessive Compulsive Disorder (OCD), bipolar disorder and a number of other developmental or non-developmental problems and most importantly, they exist in many children <u>without</u> any other diagnosis. So the myth is unknown - the child has no diagnoses but just seems off.

What are sensory processing issues? (Sensory Processing Disorder/Sensory Integration Dysfunction)

Sensory Processing Disorder is difficulty integrating the everyday sensory inputs that come into a person's system. For example, you and I may be able to hold a conversation while our kids are playing, talking and making noises in the background because you and I can "filter out" the kids' noises in the background while focusing on our conversation – parents do it all the time. A person with sensory integration issues will not be able to hold a conversation in the same situation because their internal sensory system cannot effectively "filter out" the background noises and tune in to the conversation. This is an example of an auditory processing difficulty.

There are seven areas of sensory integration, and to have an impairment in any of these areas will feel very much like your drive to the grocery store in our analogy above. Below are the seven sensory areas:

I. Proprioceptive (body awareness)
II. Vestibular (movement)
III. Tactile (touch)
IV. Auditory (sound)
V. Visual
VI. Taste
VII. Smell

The inability to filter out background noises may not seem like a big deal, but when a person's ability to process all the daily environmental stimuli in either a few, or all seven sensory areas is compromised, the mere thought of existing in this world can mean tremendous challenge to the individual depending on the severity of their sensory integration issues, again, just like your wild drive to the grocery store. For example, take a child with severe sensory integration issues who walks into a room and suddenly falls apart – he has a meltdown the size of a tornado. No one would ever guess the source of the meltdown was - that this child walked from a room with relatively flat walls to a room with a textured walls, and his compromised sensory system was unable to process the textural input of a textured wall. The offending stimuli could be that subtle in some cases where it appears that the child just suddenly freaked out "out of the blue". In other cases, it could be a buildup of various stimuli over a period of time that soon enough causes the whole sensory system to become overloaded. Unfortunately, the disintegration of the overloaded sensory system usually manifests itself behaviorally, and this sets your child right onto "the downward spiral" that will be discussed at the end of this chapter.

More on sensory integration

No one solution will fit every child with sensory integration issues. Sensory integration issues exist differently in individual children and adults, in different sensory areas and to different degrees, therefore they present themselves differently in individual children.

Children with Sensory Integration Dysfunctions can be hyposensitive (under-responsive), hypersensitive (over-responsive), or both (hyposensitive in some areas and hypersensitive in other areas) to stimuli. The above two examples (inability to filter out background noises and wall texture) are both examples of hypersensitivity – over-reacting and oversensitivity to stimuli. The hypersensitive child, who is over sensitive to tactile, visual, auditory and other stimuli will exhibit behavior indicating overloaded sensory systems. The overload will typically manifest itself in undesirable behaviors like a melt down after participating in an over stimulating activity, such as playing a videogame or watching TV.

Cases of hyposensitivity raise more sensory seeking behaviors in the child such as putting inappropriate objects in the mouth, or touching things. The hyposensitive child is under-responsive to tactile stimuli so that the child seeks more tactile input. An example could be that a child often hurts a playmate while playing because, due to his hyposensitivity/under-responsiveness, he is unable to feel his own strength.

The following is a list of **symptoms of sensory processing disorder**, and the specific sensory deficit category the symptoms indicate. There are a lot more symptoms than shown in the below list. In a later chapter, meeting the sensory needs will be addressed in much more detail.

I. Proprioceptive
   A. Uncomfortable when in close proximity to other people or uncomfortable being in crowds. Is clumsy, has poor balance, or uncoordinated
   B. Appears hyper and unsettling, or fidgeting constantly
   C. Agitated, very easily upset (or proprioceptive in combination with any of the other seven sensory areas)
   D. Has a hard time initiating tasks, is very slow in execution
   E. Plays rough and tends to always be roughhousing in his or her play

II. Tactile
   A. Constant appropriate or inappropriate touching of people, things, textures, etc.
   B. Discomfort with clothing, socks, anything that touches the skin
III. Auditory
   A. Easily distracted by background noises that others don't usually notice
IV. Visual
   A. Easily distracted by visual stimulation that others aren't bothered by
   B. Aggressive behaviors or agitation after video games, TV, or any screen exposure
V. Mix of the sensory areas
   A. Overwhelmed easily in class, playgrounds, outings, stores, etc.
   B. Acts shy, reserved, or withdrawn in social settings; has general difficulties in social settings (this could either be strictly an introverted personality trait, a result of sensory disintegration in any of the seven areas, or a combination of both personality and sensory)

In each of these seven sensory integration areas, the child can exhibit either sensory seeking or sensory avoiding behaviors. Sensory seeking behaviors/activities are an attempt by the child to get the additional sensory input his sensory system is missing and craving. Sensory avoiding behaviors/activities are an attempt to release some of the sensory system overload the child experiences.

Is it Behavioral or Sensory?

The question becomes is the exhibited issue behavioral or sensory and how do I tell which it is?

Continuing with our previous wild drive to the grocery store analogy. While all the drivers around you may think that your driving behaviors are very inappropriate, and are honking their horns at you, if you have earmuffs on you won't hear the horns. Not until you take your earmuffs off will you clearly hear someone honking at you and be able to take action to get out of someone else's space. Better yet, also cleaning your windshield will help see more clearly so you can stay in your own lane. Relieving your leg from the numbness will help you put the right amount of force onto the gas pedal at the right time to better control your speed. There is no doubt that your overall driving behavior will improve after you address the compromised sensory input because all your poor driving behaviors are sensory-induced. We aim to meet a child's needs, starting with sensory needs, to reduce a large amount of behavior problems that are sensory induced behaviors.

Only after we clear up all the items compromising your hearing, sight and tactile input can you properly orient yourself and start driving appropriately. But, can we expect your driving behavior to be perfect? Not necessarily. Some people will still get into other people's space, cut people off, or speed and it has nothing to do with how well they are able to orient themselves with their surroundings. This is when you treat the behavior rather than the sensory needs. But you won't succeed very well trying to treat the behaviors if you don't have sensory needs addressed, just like getting a speeding ticket won't help you slow down if your leg is still all numb and you can't tell whether you're stomping onto the gas pedal or barely touching it. Behind every behavior problem there is a reason, if not sensory or unmet needs (such as your windshield being muddy), then some other underlying reasons (such as you being late to a job interview and being in a real rush to speed). You want to peel the onion and address each behavior appropriately at the proper layer.

Every time you see a child exhibiting behavior that seems off, there usually is a reason behind it. It could be one of several reasons or a mix of reasons:

1) A sensory issue manifested behaviorally. This was explained in the above example where a child's sensory challenges (sensory overstimulation or under stimulation) are manifested behaviorally. This is where you are speeding because your leg is all numb and you don't know that your foot is forcing onto the gas pedal so hard.
2) A behavioral problem with underlying issues. For example, behaviors with the purpose of gaining access to something he desires, or avoid something undesirable, or to get attention, etc. This is where you are speeding because you are late to your job interview or because you just got a new car and it feels so good to fly your new baby down the street.
3) Unrealistic expectations - it could simply be that the expectation made on the child is beyond what a child can attain. This is where you turn onto the wrong street because you are in the foreign country and to

expect you to find the right street when you can't even read the street name on the sign is unrealistic. An obvious real life example of unrealistic expectations is a 3 year old making noises, running all over the place during a symphony performance and behaving "inappropriately" because the expectation for a 3-year-old to sit through a 2 hour symphony is simply unrealistic. When a child fails to perform, we do need to examine what it is we are asking of the child.

If your child exhibits some of the above symptoms of a child with SDN, read the later chapter on meeting the sensory needs to better understand and get practical strategies to help promote a more functional sensory system. You can also have your child evaluated by an Occupational Therapist to see if your child has Sensory Integration Dysfunction (Sensory Processing Disorder). One of my following chapters in this book provides specific strategies on meeting a child's sensory and internal needs. If your child does have sensory issues, some of his behaviors may be sensory induced, some may be strictly behavioral issues, or they may be a combination of both. Sometimes it's clear, yet sometimes it's unknown until you test it out and play with it to fully understand what is causing the behavior.

For a child with sensory issues, your triage process is this: Ensure that you meet the child's sensory needs (I provide some strategies in a later chapter) and meet them at the right time, before you try too hard to address the behavior issues. If the child's sensory needs are met and the behavior is still there, address the issue behaviorally - success paradigm is very helpful for that, and the later behavioral strategies are very useful for that too. Many times it's a mix and you need to address both. Later chapters of this book will show you how to address the issues from the sensory perspective and from the behavior perspective.

Timing is extremely important in addressing any behavior. You will learn why in a later chapter where I explain the behavior ABCs.

Treating sensory needs is different than treating behavior and you need to address each one with the proper timing. Section III, Meeting Internal Needs, discusses in more detail how to meet your child's sensory needs as one of the internal needs. Section IV, Transforming External Behaviors, provides details on modifying your child's behaviors. It is important that you read both of those sections to fully understand the differences and approaches to address both the sensory needs and behaviors. You have to be careful not to inadvertently reinforce the undesirable behavior while trying to address the sensory needs.

The Downward Spiral

Sensory dysfunction can cause the very terrible downward spiral that I briefly mentioned earlier. Here are the details on how the downward spiral works. A downward spiral initiated from sensory disintegration and manifested through lack of proper support is exactly what was going on with our classic Theater Child (from Chapter 1). Here is an explanation of the downward spiral:

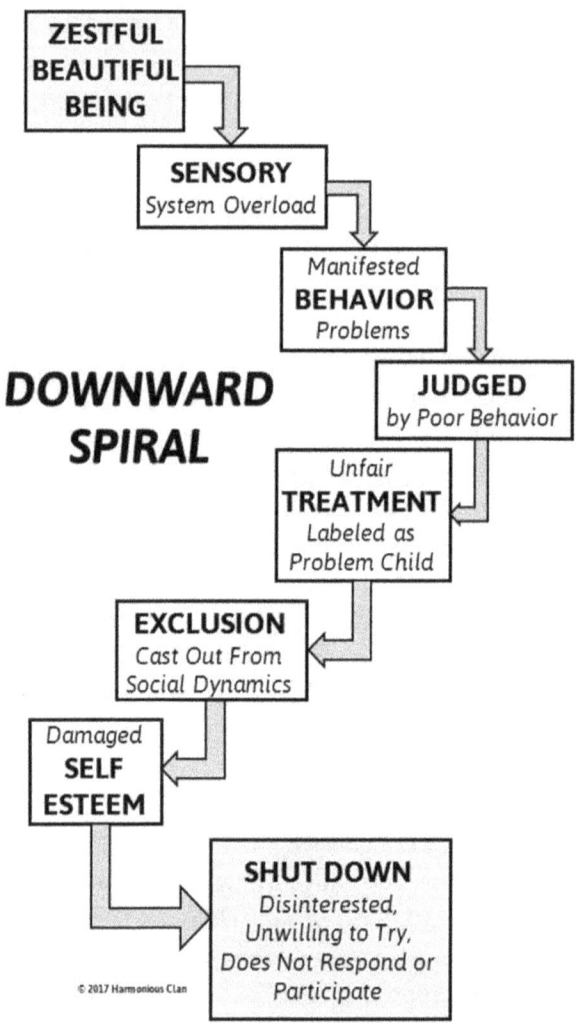

Figure 3-2 Typical Downward Behavior Spiral

The child is a well-spirited beautiful being possibly with multiple talents like our Theater Child. The child's sensory system gets overloaded with daily environmental stimuli (noise, people, lights), whatever is going on in the room or environment. The child's overloaded system manifests itself behaviorally, and sadly enough, the child is judged by his outward behavior, even when the behavior is due to the child's challenged sensory system. The judgement leads to the others treating the child as "a problem" instead of a unique beautiful being who needs, desires and deserves understanding, acceptance, support, and fundamental fairness. An example of the unfair treatment due to judgement is when the theater teacher immediately pulled our Theater Child out of the class and said nothing about the child who initiated the disturbance by smacking our Theater Child in the face. Is that fair? No, especially not from the Theater Child's perspective. Now that someone has labeled the child as "a problem", naturally, he is excluded from the group activities and the whole group's social dynamics. As discussed in our earlier chapter, this was when our Theater Child was given no lines in the play, and no spot on stage during the group dance and performance. To be excluded from the group where you are and deemed that you "don't belong here" is a tremendous loneliness for the child. The heart that clamors for a sense of belonging and a sense of home is answered instead with exclusion, unfair and unsupported treatment that places upon the child an unfair label that "you are not good enough to be here". The child is thinking, "But everybody else IS good enough to be here, except for me". The child's self-worth and self-esteem are damaged, having evaporated from the experience and is now non-existent. Before you know it, the child shuts down. This is demonstrated by the behavior of our Theater Child by day 5 where he is seen sitting in the far corner of the room, with no line, no spot on stage, no costume, nothing but a drawing pad and a crayon with his head down deep into his drawing pad. He is in total silence, totally disconnected with his surroundings; he is sensing profound loneliness and indignity. He is shrinking himself into as small of a ball as he can be as he feels he neither belongs nor is he good enough to be there. The Theater Child is now in total isolation where no one can reach or break through no matter how hard they try. The theater child has been shunned and excluded from the one activity in which he so longed to participate.

How did our well-spirited being spiral down to a tiny little ball in a corner? Originated from sensory overload and furthered down by an unawareness and unwillingness from others to support the "problem child", the downward spiral accelerated. It was a heartbreaking process to watch as I stood on the side to witness my own baby fall into this downward spiral. I wish for no child to be in this predicament. This book is here to intervene at every turn in the downward spiral, to give practical strategies and to empower you to pick your child right off the spiral (wherever he is in the spiral), raise him above all the obstacles to a place where he is living out his beauty and spirit as he was created. When he is raised above all obstacles and he is empowered and supported, he is home (certainly finally having a sense of belonging), he is happy, he is flourishing and living his life as intended. He has transformed from outcast to outstanding.

◆ ◆ ◆ ◆ ◆ ◆ ◆ ◆ ◆ ◆ ◆ ◆ ◆ ◆ ◆ ◆

Your Take-away from this chapter:

- ✓ A child with Sensitive Divergent Needs behaviors are only artifacts of his/her internal chaotic state due to sensory system deficits
- ✓ Address the internal needs so that you are well positioned to transform your child's external behaviors, and bring your child from chaos to harmony. Read on to learn how

◆ ◆ ◆ ◆ ◆ ◆ ◆ ◆ ◆ ◆ ◆ ◆ ◆ ◆ ◆ ◆

Section II - Success Paradigm: Sowing the Seeds

CHAPTER 4
The Game Plan That Fuels Outstanding Behaviors

♦ ♦ ♦ ♦ ♦ ♦ ♦ ♦ ♦ ♦ ♦ ♦ ♦ ♦ ♦ ♦

What You Will Learn In This Chapter:

- ✓ What shapes a child's behaviors
- ✓ The #1 foundation for transforming a child's behavior - "Success Paradigm"
- ✓ 4 Strategies to give your child a success paradigm and ignite the behavioral transformation process

♦ ♦ ♦ ♦ ♦ ♦ ♦ ♦ ♦ ♦ ♦ ♦ ♦ ♦ ♦ ♦

What shapes a child's behaviors?

Suppose you take freeway 8 to work and you hit traffic. You take freeway 8 for several days in a row and you hit bad traffic every time you are on that freeway. Your thoughts say that you don't have time to be on freeway 8. The thought that you don't have time to sit in traffic gives you upset feelings when you are rushing to work. This upset feeling will then form your behavior of exploring alternative routes to work. The idea that thoughts shape feelings and feelings shape behaviors come from Cognitive Behavioral Therapy (CBT) which is an effective method to treat patients with mental and emotional distress, by changing their thoughts, therefore feelings and behaviors.

Once you establish your thoughts and feelings, which then establish your behavior, your behavior won't change. Your behavior will only change if your thoughts and feelings change. For example, if you change your thought from "I don't have time to sit on freeway 8" to "I have more time to listen to my favorite program in the car", then your feeling changes from one of upset to one of content. If you feel content, you may reconsider staying with freeway 8. The key is to change your thoughts, which change your feelings, which change your behaviors. See figure 4-1.

The child with SDN tends to not think and feel the best about himself. This is the case because his experiences about himself haven't been great and successful experiences. We know that a child with SDN tends to spend a lot of time being in trouble in school and failing his parents' expectations at home. The figure below illustrates how a child goes from failure experiences, to the thought that "I'm not good enough", to feeling of inept, and finally to behaving like they are "bad kids". The

What Shapes a Child's Behavior?

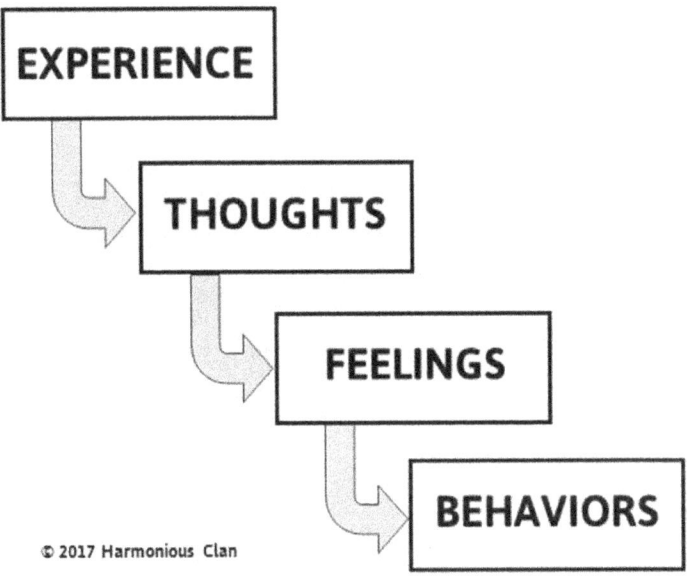

Figure 4-1 What Shapes a Child's Behavior?

child's thought process is this: Every time I step onto the soccer field I end up hitting and kicking my teammates, I never kick the ball when I'm supposed to and I end up getting pulled off the field for my bad behaviors; I'm not good enough to play with my team. It's a cycle because the more the child behaves like a "bad kid" the more failures he will experience, and the more poorly he will feel about himself. See figure 4-2.

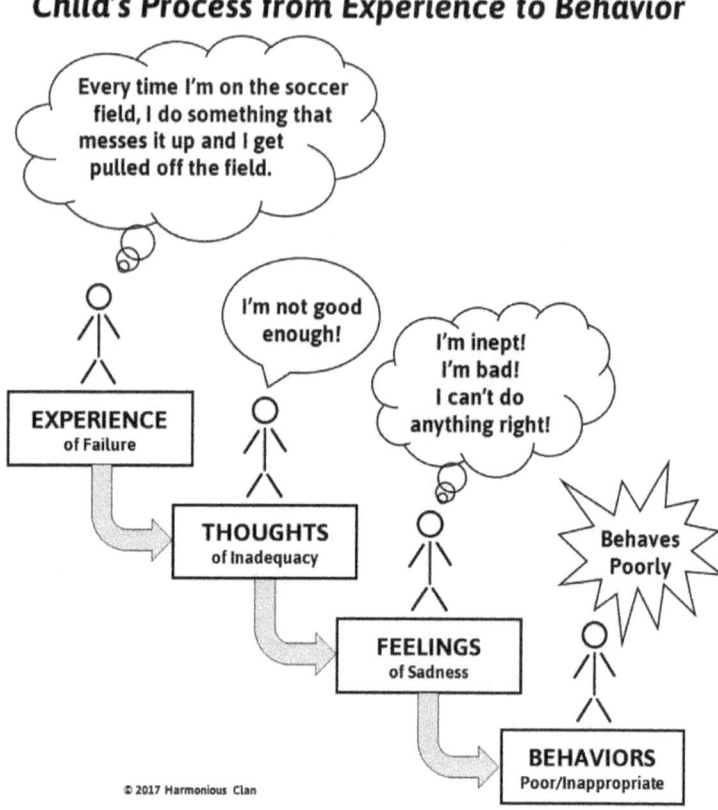

Figure 4-2 Child's Process from Experience to Behavior

I have found that when you change the child's experiences, you can actually change his thoughts, feelings, and ultimately, his behaviors.

Let's go back to our theater camp child (Ch 1 & 2), his experience is failure everywhere he goes. The theater camp is only a sample of his experience. For these children that we are discussing, this failure in the child's experience is everywhere - at school, at home, at camp, at soccer, you name it. As if the child's own personal experiences of failure aren't enough (internal experiences), they also experience negative judgement from others (external experiences) that really crush their self-worth. Through all these unsuccessful **experiences**, the child formulates his **thinking** in his heart that "I'm not good at anything; I'm a failure". How does this thinking form the child's feeling? They feel like a failure, they feel poorly about themselves, they feel like a bad person, like an unworthy person. And no doubt they behave the same way they feel – like a bad person, like an unworthy person, like a person who does no good to the society. The child's thinking about himself drives his behavior and is based on his external and internal experiences.

Now you want to change the child's poor behavior? Really? You want to change a behavior that is rooted in that many layers of "solid cognitive foundation"? You are going to have to start working from the very first layer even before thoughts formulation - their experiences. You must change one layer at a time focusing first on their **experiences**, then their **thinking** and their **feeling**, before you hit their **behavior**. That's right! If you can **break down that pyramid and rebuild that foundation again**, see Figure 4-3, then when you get to the top of the pyramid you will see that dramatic day-and-night difference in their behavior in the most positive way. Absolutely doable! And I am here to teach you how. Read on.

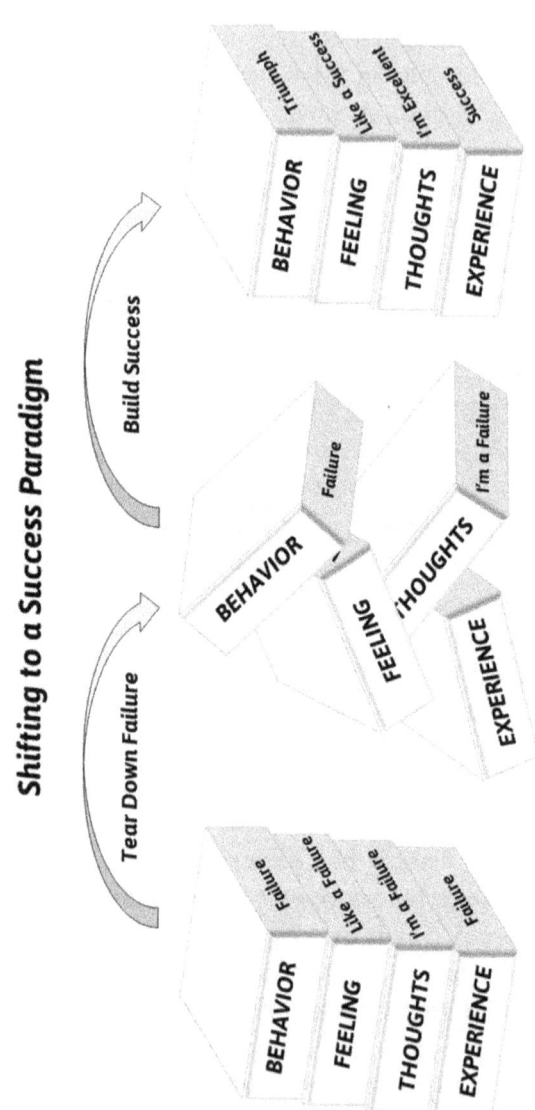

Figure 4-3 Shifting to a Success Paradigm

The Success Paradigm

Imagine if you can give the child with SDN the gift of a success paradigm, which immediately changes his experience from failure to success. Would he start thinking and feeling good enough, not based on anyone else's approval, but solely based on *his own experience* of success? If he starts feeling like a winner, wouldn't he act like a winner? This paradigm shift, the gift of a success paradigm, is a gift of triumph and ignition for the child.

The success paradigm is when you reprogram a child's experience from one of failure to one of success. If he can step onto the soccer field feeling "I'm a great teammate", his behavior will be more appropriate. He is going to step onto the soccer field without hitting another child. He may even decide to participate and kick the ball like he is supposed to. It's a paradigm shift, as illustrated in Figure 4-3.

This is why it's important to change the child's experience by helping him have a paradigm shift in his experience. We do this by creating little successes. Notice I said "create". The successes are most likely not there and they most likely won't be there unless you "create" them. You may be thinking, but these kids really fail at everything; they really behave so poorly; there is nearly not a single minute that they are doing something right. If you are a parent of a child with SDN, you will know what I mean. You may feel so frustrated that it almost feels like you are nagging him every minute that you are with him. It's time to change that self-defeating experience for both you and your child. However, the child isn't the one to initiate the change, rather, the adult is the one to initiate the change;

the adult is the one to create something out of nothing for the child so that his experience is a successful one.

How? I'll give you four strategies to create little successes:

Strategy 1: Catch them being good (catch them not being bad)
Strategy 2: Artificially create the success
Strategy 3: Create incremental successes
Strategy 4: Do not ask them to do anything they cannot succeed in during the success paradigm shifting stage

Strategy 1: Catch them being good (catch them being not bad)

If your child is always bothering his sister, for example, you are not going to tell him to "be nice to your sister" and wait for him to go out of his way and do something nice before you acknowledge him. You basically need to capture moments when he is not instigating something towards his sister and say "Great job, you are not bothering your sister. You could have and that would have been a lot more fun for you, but you didn't. You chose to sit here on the couch. I'm so proud of you!" "Look at you! You are sitting so nicely with your hands in your lap while your sister plays nearby. I am so proud of how beautifully you are sitting with your hands to yourself". Guess what you have just done? In that moment, you have created an experience of success for your child. The reality is that he is just vegetating on the couch and doing nothing, but you are acknowledging his success of not bothering his sister. Instead of experiencing a failure, which is "I'm always an instigator. My parents are always condemning me..." He is experiencing success – "wow, look at me! I'm not an instigator. I can leave my sister alone. I'm great and my parents noticed too!" By keeping with and repeating the desired behaviors, you strengthen that in your child. The behavior we want to select becomes the focus instead of the maladaptive behavior that is missing.

No matter how chaotic the day may be, you can certainly find moments when your child is not doing something bad and really acknowledge that – "Look at you, you are relaxing" "You're not having a tantrum", "you're not creating a mess here". You will be amazed at the how much you noticing and acknowledging the 'good' (non bad) behaviors will impact your child's future behaviors. Try it out today! (If using language sounds unfamiliar, strange, or contradicting to you, please refer to Chapter 6, The Language That Elates & Elevates Your Child, to learn more).

Strategy 2: Artificially create the success

Children with behavior challenges aren't going to just experience a big load of success on their own. We have to go out of our way to create the success for them. As a parent or caregiver, we have to be the ignition to their success paradigm. Here is an example of what I mean – to my most defiant son who is so stubborn that he never wants to do anything that I tell him to do, compliance is not a strength. I strategically set up compliance exercises that create little successes for him:

> I asked him to go to the kitchen counter, get my white bowl and take a few bites of the cookie inside the

bowl. My son did _exactly as I said_, which is unusual. I immediately cheered him on with excitement, "Wow, look at you! You did EXACTLY what I told you to do! You're great at obeying your parents!" But you know what really happened. What child will refuse to eat a cookie when asked? While I do not promote sweets for children, I am trying to make a point here that this situation was a "set up" because I'm giving him credit for something that no child would refuse to do. Now do you see what I mean by "creating" little successes? You must "create" these scenarios, almost "artificially", if need be, to elevate your child's successful experiences. It really doesn't matter what the actual experience is so long he walks out of the interaction feeling successful. By doing a few of these exercises each day, you are re-writing your child's life story from one of failure to one of success. You are erasing the past image of himself and creating a success paradigm for your child. This success paradigm, once created, will transform your child's behavior inside out.

Here is a second example on artificially creating success:

I was trying to teach one of my sons the concept that "I can wait to do what I want to do". Most times this child gets very upset when he is doing something or wanting to do something and I pull him back to get his clothes folded or finish a task, for example. He started getting a very bad attitude when I asked him to do that. What did I do? I started talking to him about the concept that I can wait to do what I want to do, and I can do what my parents are asking me to do first. One time all the children were rushing to the backyard to play and of course he was eager to go, too. I stopped him and asked "could you please go get our baby brother a little snack?" The background here is that he loves his baby brother and he loves feeling big by doing things only adults do, such as getting the snack for the baby (due to choking hazard, only adults are allowed to get our baby a snack in our house). So he didn't stumble at all. He immediately got a cup and poured some crackers out to give to the baby. He was feeling big. Right away, with all my energy, I said "What a great job you did. Instead of rushing to the backyard to play, you stopped to do exactly what I asked you to do while everyone was already playing outside." Again, this is a bit of a set up because taking care of his baby brother is something he loves to do and not something he would ever say no to.

You know your child well and you need to use that knowledge to create those situations, like above, where your child can have a great success. Then you want to celebrate it big time. In my son's mind, what is he learning? He is building his experience of success. He is experiencing the actual fact that "yes, I can wait to do what I want to do! I can do what my parents ask me instead and I don't have to be anxious about my own agenda. I don't have to get upset when my parents stop me to do something else." It was a bit of a setup and a trick, but it really doesn't matter – if you don't have enough successes you have to fake some – fake it until you make it!

You must ignite in his mind these small successes, so he has something upon which to build. What would your child's reaction be when you do that? "For one time you are not upset with me!" My son was so proud looking at me with his big shiny eyes "yeah, I'm so proud. I can stop and do what you ask me to do!" He was so happy. But that wasn't it. After that event, I continued to create these little successes out of nothing everywhere I could. After a while I had that behavior fixed, his image of himself now says "I'm a successful person" and he started behaving that way.

Strategy 3: Create incremental success

Many times we ask our children to do things that involve way too many steps, and if they don't make it through all the steps they get no credit. For example, clean your room, get ready for school and meet me in the car.... These things take a lot of steps if you really look at it closely. When we are talking about a child with SDN, there are many things going on internally for him that cause these simple tasks to become so difficult. If he fails in any one of these steps he doesn't get partial credit. In the end you're yelling at him out of frustration, and he is feeling like a failure, like he can't even do such a simple task. That's not a good feeling for him.

You need to start off by breaking the task down to very small increments where there is no one step he couldn't do.

Example 1: Clean up your room. That is actually a big task – how many corners and spots are there in a room? Break it down to incremental tasks such that it's no longer such an overwhelming big task.

> First ask him to go pick up 5 items. That's pretty simple. His mind starts getting focused into counting the 5 items, which is quick. He comes back saying he did it, and you celebrate like there is no tomorrow, "Yay! You did it! I told you to pick up 5 things and you did exactly that!" You should also give him a token at that time. We will talk about the token system in a later chapter, but right now we need to focus on building that success paradigm. Then you tell him, "I wonder if you can pick up 10 items this time. You were so successful with 5 items that I think you are able to undertake a much bigger challenge. Count 10 things and come back to me". They are running back to their room all pumped up "yes, I can surely do 10!" They pick up 10 and come back to you – fabulous cheers again, here is another token for you. Now you ask him to go pick up 15 items, but from my experience, by the third time around the child comes back cheering, "Mama, I picked up 45 things in my room!" and they are so happy. You celebrate again "Wow, I had only asked you to pick up 15 and you picked up 45! I'm so impressed with what you did!" If you weren't on the cheerleading team in high school, get on with the program and be a cheerleader now! Your child needs you to be that cheerleader.

That's a lot of success experiences right there. From my experience with Children with SDN, had you asked your child the traditional way "go clean up your room", not only would he dawdle, even if he did start the task, something upsetting would happen during the process of cleaning. He most likely would not have experienced these 3-4 rounds of successes, and he would have lost the experience of success and the ignition of excellence in himself.

Strategy 4: Do not ask them to do anything they cannot succeed in during the success paradigm shifting stage

You want to make sure that every step that you ask him to do is something he can certainly do and do well. Do not ask him to do anything that he cannot do, at least not in the success paradigm shifting stage. Building upon the existing successes and pushing him beyond that point is something separate from the success paradigm shift and there is a place for that, but not here, not when you are trying to give your child a paradigm shift into the success paradigm.

◆ ◆ ◆ ◆ ◆ ◆ ◆ ◆ ◆ ◆ ◆ ◆ ◆ ◆ ◆ ◆

Your Take-Away From This Chapter:

✓ *In order to transform a child's behavior, you must start from changing his/her experiences*

- ✓ Providing your child a "success paradigm" shift is the first step to address unwanted behaviors
- ✓ "Success paradigm" changes the child's image of himself from one of failure to one of success by strategically creating little successes that otherwise wouldn't have existed

◆ ◆ ◆ ◆ ◆ ◆ ◆ ◆ ◆ ◆ ◆ ◆ ◆ ◆ ◆

CHAPTER 5

The Energy Shift That Transforms the Failure Cycle to the Success Cycle

◆ ◆ ◆ ◆ ◆ ◆ ◆ ◆ ◆ ◆ ◆ ◆ ◆ ◆ ◆ ◆ ◆

What You Will Learn In This Chapter:

- ✓ Where is your energy going, and why does it matter?
- ✓ The energy-behavior cycle
- ✓ How to turn a failure energy-behavior cycle into successful energy-behavior cycle

◆ ◆ ◆ ◆ ◆ ◆ ◆ ◆ ◆ ◆ ◆ ◆ ◆ ◆ ◆ ◆ ◆

Where is your energy going, and why does it matter?

As discussed, a typical child with SDN has a historical experience as a failure due to his condition-induced behaviors. The "success paradigm" in the last chapter changes the child's image of himself from one of failure to one of success by strategically creating little successes that otherwise wouldn't have existed. This chapter introduces you to a technique built upon the success paradigm idea - being incredibly excited about their *"not-so-bad" behavior*. By "not-so-bad" behavior, I'm referring to a behavior that's not exactly the fantastic behavior you ultimately want, but it is incrementally better than a "bad behavior" that you are trying to avoid. For example, if you ultimately want <u>sharing</u> with a friend, but the child frequently <u>hits</u> a friend, then you don't wait for the <u>sharing</u> to happen before you celebrate the child, because the sharing may never happen on its own. You want to catch the moment when the child is just <u>sitting</u> next to a friend without hitting the friend and celebrate – "fantastic job sitting next to Jason keeping your hands to yourself!" The incremental effort (the 2 minutes of sitting without hitting) even though isn't all the way up to <u>sharing</u>, is at least one, if not several, notches up from the <u>hitting</u> already – so celebrate it.

If you don't see any excellent behavior in the moment, celebrate the *"not so bad" behavior*. The child with SDN experiences a lot of emotions from you during their failures. "How many times have I told you not to do ___?" "This is the worst thing you could do!" Those are common experiences they have. When they do something wrong, your emotions are big and strong, and the child with SDN can sense it a mile away. Children are made to draw your energy and the child with SDN can sense where your energy is more so than their peers. They gravitate towards your energy.

The energy-behavior cycle
If they can sense those moments when your energy is focused on their failure, they can sense that you are exerting the

strongest emotions you have. They have just done something terrible and you are frustrated, so enraged, that you are at your wits end. You don't know what to do with them. You may not even know what to do with yourself. They see it. They feel it all. They are sensitive and in-tune with where you are emotionally. They will do more of what caused your rage to draw more of your strong emotions, even though children are not evil and are not out to get you. They just simply gravitate towards where your energy is. If they feel that in their failure is where your emotions and energies are, then they will subconsciously gravitate towards more failure. Now both you and your child are in the downward cycle (see figure 5-1).

You can stop this cycle by shifting more of your energy into success. In the "success paradigm" chapter, I shared how you create little successes. You need to create these little successes so they can get a sense of where your fire is. By doing so, you have ignited a little bit of that success; next you set the whole field on fire for triumph by pouring all your positive energy and emotions into their successes. The child with SDN will sense your positive energy vested in their successes when you become incredibly excited about their "not so bad" behaviors. That's right - I didn't say their "good behaviors"; instead I said their "adaptive" behaviors, because if you wait for their good behaviors you'll wait so long that you lose all your momentum and you don't get enough opportunities to pour your positive energy.

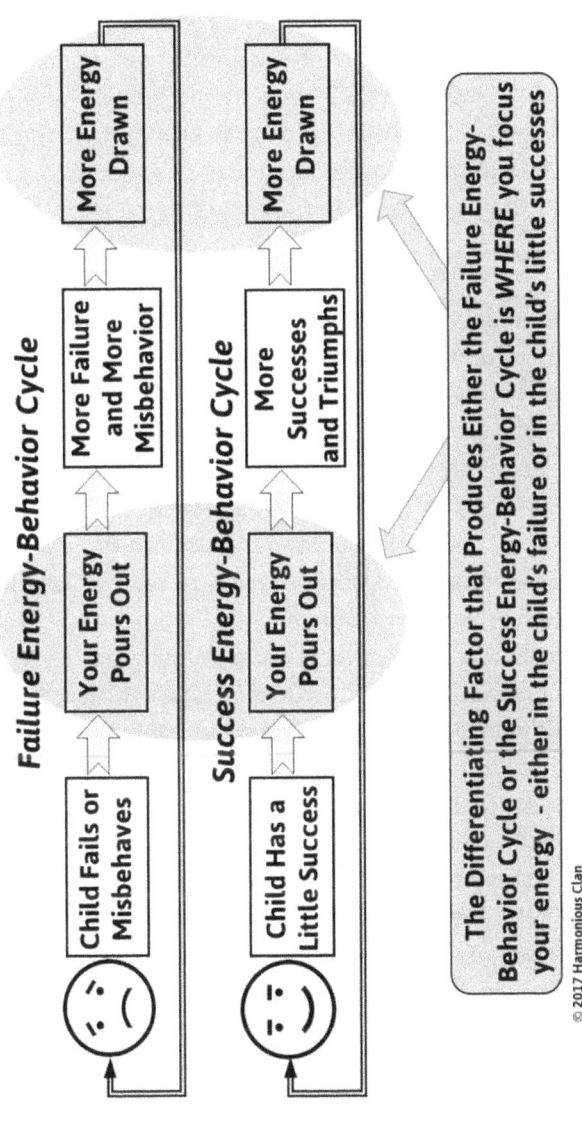

Figure 5-1 Energy Behavior Cycle

Think of a time when a child has failed your expectations. How strong was your emotion? How strong was your energy of anger and disappointment? Mine could be very strong sometimes. Multiply the intensity of that energy by 5 times, and put that energy right into your child's "not so bad" behavior. Celebrate the "not so bad" behaviors to no end. Here is an example.

One of my many Children with SDN had a very hard time with transitions. During transition times such as getting into the car to go out, he used to always step on or hit his siblings when everyone is putting their shoes on and getting into the car buckling up. The expectation in our clan of five-close-in-age young children is to get your own shoes on and help a young one with their shoes, get a young child into the car and help them buckle. Imagine 3 buckles each car seat, which meant 15 buckles before we could drive and at the time only 1.5 children could buckle themselves. That's not counting the 20 socks plus 10 shoes that had to go onto 10 feet, out of which only two children could complete the job independently. I was busy every time we tried to get out. Instead of waiting for a "good behavior" such as getting his own shoes on and helping another young child, I celebrated the "not so bad" behavior - the first second he stepped foot into the garage and didn't step on anyone (not yet). "Wow, you kept your hands and feet to yourself and I can see you're headed exactly where you are supposed to get shoes on! I know just how much more fun it would have been for you to step on your brother and watch him get upset, but you chose not to and I'm proud of you. I can just see how much self-control and kindness you have in your heart." Even if he was just about to go step on a brother, he wouldn't want to anymore after hearing what I said. Had I waited another second while I took care of another child he would have stepped on someone already and I would have lost my chance to celebrate his "not so bad" behavior of simply walking into the garage. Simply walking into the garage doesn't sound grand at all; it's not like he got all his siblings shoes on and buckled them in addition to buckling himself, but he could have hit or stepped on someone and he didn't. So I celebrated with all my energy. Just think about <u>the kind of energy you have from your worst rage, flip the energy into positive, and multiply the intensity by 10 times</u>, and there you have it. That is the energy your child needs to receive from you in order to ignite his/her passion for triumph, which clings onto your own energy.

The idea of this strategy is to make your child feel where your fire is. They need to feel that your fire is focused on their success. You want to continue to use the success paradigm strategy in the previous chapter to create more of those little successes that are easy for your child to achieve, and then you want to use the strategy in this chapter to really celebrate that. Show them that you are all about their success. Once they have experienced the success you have created for them, and they have experienced that your fire is in their success, you have not only ignited, but empowered, your child to live for triumph. You have set the child on fire for achieving more success. Now, not only have they experienced the success, their thoughts are telling them "I can do it! I can be successful", and their behaviors will dramatically improve because of their experiences and thoughts. All of a sudden, they want to go back and create more of those successful experiences for themselves, and the experience they create will lead to thoughts of triumph, which will lead to outstanding behaviors. This is how you turn a downward spiral of poor behaviors and poor self-image into an upward spiral of child-initiating, innate desire and ability to succeed.

◆ ◆ ◆ ◆ ◆ ◆ ◆ ◆ ◆ ◆ ◆ ◆ ◆ ◆ ◆ ◆ ◆

Your Take-Away From This Chapter:

- ✓ Be 10 times more intense and energetic about your child's "not so bad" behaviors than you are about his worst doings
- ✓ Tell your child "I am ON FIRE for your success" by exerting your intense energy in the right places

◆ ◆ ◆ ◆ ◆ ◆ ◆ ◆ ◆ ◆ ◆ ◆ ◆ ◆ ◆ ◆ ◆

CHAPTER 6
The Language that Elates & Elevates Your Child

♦ ♦ ♦ ♦ ♦ ♦ ♦ ♦ ♦ ♦ ♦ ♦ ♦ ♦ ♦

What You Will Learn In This Chapter:

✓ How to speak truth, power, and success into your child's heart that will transform his/her behaviors

♦ ♦ ♦ ♦ ♦ ♦ ♦ ♦ ♦ ♦ ♦ ♦ ♦ ♦ ♦

How to make your words more impactful for your child?

Children with SDN have a lot stacked against them both internally and externally that makes everything much more difficult for them. Internally they have sensory difficulties; neurologically some things work differently than in typical children; their executive functioning is difficult and a struggle. The whole world seems to be against them because no one understands what they feel and why they do the things they do. No one understands how hard they are trying to be good and no one understands their world. They have so much going against them that it seems difficult to put enough greatness into their lives. This is why you really need to feed the child with more and more encouragements for successes. You need to put more fire onto the success that you ignited through the strategies in the previous chapter.

Now that we showed you how to ignite the success paradigm in your child in the previous chapter and you have started that process, in this chapter we'll discuss how to take it a step further simply with your words. Below is a helpful format on how to charge your words with the power of success for your child:

1) **Narrate in detail to the child the exact action your child just did.**
2) **Describe the lesser action he could have taken instead of the greater action he actually took.**
3) **Acknowledge his effort by pointing out that what he did was not easy.**
4) **Tell your child how much you appreciate what he did and how awesome he is.**
5) **Give them the benefit of the doubt, and assume the best of them** - this is very powerful!

The success strategies in the previous chapter will give your child that new success paradigm he needs, and many of the undesirable behaviors will diminish through that process. You've ignited the success, and now you're going to fire it up even more.

I want to clarify the number 2 above – why would anyone ever want to mention a lesser action to a child? We are speaking in a language that elevates your child, aren't we, so why would you want the mention of a lesser action in your language? As a general rule, I never would. In this context, though, my specific reason for mentioning the lesser action is to **point out to the child the transformation he or she has made**, which in itself is very encouraging realization for them. It's like drawing a growth chart on the wall to show your child how much he or she has grown in the last year. You're applauding him for choosing the high road and acknowledging him for consciously saying no to the lesser choices. In my years of experience, children are amused to see what you are saying here. You will see this in my example below. However, each child is different. If you find that this lesser statement, that was meant to be a show of transformation for the child, is starting to serve as catalyst for child to suddenly behave poorly like he used to, then ignore number/step 2 (Describe the lesser action) and only highlight the positive (step 1 plus all of the remaining steps).

Here is an example:

> Let's go back to the previous example of my child having a hard time with transitions, but this time, doing this case study in the context of how your words can have a huge impact on the situation. With a family of five children, transitions are even more difficult for him due to the number of siblings. To recap, during transitions, such as getting into the car when the family is

going out, switching from playing to dining, etc., he would get silly, misbehave, hit a sibling, step on someone, be inappropriately loud, etc.

In the previous chapter, I caught my son going into the garage to put his shoes on for a family outing and as soon as he stepped his foot into the garage without hitting anybody, I immediately jumped in with my cheers. Had I waited another 5 minutes, he would have had already the chance to hit one of his siblings. But no, I took the very first opportunity I could to catch him being good. That was the concept from the last chapter.

The strategy from this chapter is about how you use your words. The following example would be discussed in one statement with your child. The brackets text sections are references to the above stated 5 context areas you want to cover with your child during the discussion.

[1. Narrate in detail to the child the exact action your child just did.] I said, "Wow, LOOK AT YOU! You are not doing any of that! You just walked into the garage, got your socks from the basket and you were just about to sit down and focus on putting your socks on.

[2. Describe the lesser action he could have taken instead of the greater action he actually took.] Do you remember when you used to come to the garage and hit somebody, kick somebody, or step on somebody when we're transitioning into the car? You could

have done any of that to make things more fun for you, but you didn't.
[3. Acknowledge his effort by pointing out that what he did was not easy.] I know how hard it is to control your impulses to have some fun bugging your brothers, but you did it.
[4. Tell your child how much you appreciate what he did and how awesome he is.] I am so impressed with you, and I really appreciate you making the effort to be successful. And I bet you are probably thinking of helping someone else put their socks on as soon as you are done with your own!
[5. Give them the benefit of the doubt, and assume the best of them.] I am so proud of you. Do you see the difference in yourself? You have really matured."

Can you imagine how my son felt hearing that? This meant so much to my son. How he felt was so important, because feelings shape behaviors. I'm sure if your boss said this to you it would also mean a lot to you. It would definitely drive your desire to continue to outperform in your job. Everyone wants to and needs to be appreciated.

"What made you change and mature?"
This is another strategy you can use because when you ask them, it gives them a chance to reflect. While you are pumping up all his successes, he is thinking "I'm so successful, I'm being interviewed for my success recipe…" I've actually had children articulating to me exactly what they did to improve themselves. Some answers I've heard: "I've really set my mind

on being successful." "I just didn't think that was the right thing to do, and I really just wanted to do the right thing". I've even had children tell me what their success recipe is and we went on writing down his success recipe so he can reproduce success from it and other siblings can also learn from it. We have narrated together how he has overcome his challenges.

This process allows a child to create his own success recipe – how powerful is it that a child can take his success into his own hands with his own recipe? It also allows a child to reflect on his change, which builds more success under his belt to see how far he has come.

Their faces shine with a big smile because they start seeing their transformation. They look back at the days when they used to behave so poorly under the same circumstance and they laugh about it. They are so excited. Your verbal acknowledgements and your words can mean so much to them. Your words are so important to them that you need to be intentional about what you say to them.

Another example:

> One of my sons was playing with a sibling when he looked at the younger siblings' blocks and wanted to have them. Again, immediately, before he took them away from the younger sibling, I caught him being good for the one second and I jumped on it. I said, "Wow, I saw your eyes on those blocks and I knew you wanted to have them, but you didn't take them away from her". I added a lot more details, "Do you

remember when you used to just take it away and add so much chaos causing others to cry and be sad? But look at you right now. You are just looking at it and I can see it in your eyes that you're trying to think of ways to remedy your situation. You are not going to take the pieces out of her hands no matter how much you want them. You could have taken them right out of her hands and have just what you wanted, but you chose not to. You also could have yelled at her so she would give it to you, but you didn't either. You could have hit her in the head, so she'd fall and leave the pieces to you, but you didn't either."

You think of all the worst possible things your child could have done and didn't do. You detail everything he is doing right to him.

Notice I'm spending several minutes lifting up a child for his one second of pause (looked at the block). Most people, especially with a child with SDN's poor behavior track record, would have assumed this child is about to grab the pieces from the younger sibling, which could very well be true. But you must assume the best and give him that success like I did in my example.

You need to be like a sports reporter that narrates the move in slow motion to the audience. You do that to your child and your child will feel like a super star. He will be so happy to be the sports star or movie star you are narrating about. It matters to the children the 30 seconds that they didn't do something wrong and you noticed. In our house where we have five children and two adults, attention is no commodity. So if anyone gets any attention for something, it is truly huge for them. This is true even if you only have one child, he or she still desires your attention. You need to show them that even the smallest thing they do is so big to you.

◆ ◆ ◆ ◆ ◆ ◆ ◆ ◆ ◆ ◆ ◆ ◆ ◆ ◆ ◆ ◆ ◆

Your Take-Away From This Chapter:

- ✓ Your words are so powerful - use them effectively to speak to your child's heart
- ✓ Use the strategies in this chapter to make sure you are hitting the mark with your words

◆ ◆ ◆ ◆ ◆ ◆ ◆ ◆ ◆ ◆ ◆ ◆ ◆ ◆ ◆ ◆ ◆

Section III - Meeting Internal Needs: Tending the Seedlings

CHAPTER 7
The Surprising Actions That Dramatically Influence and Improve Behaviors

◆ ◆ ◆ ◆ ◆ ◆ ◆ ◆ ◆ ◆ ◆ ◆ ◆ ◆ ◆ ◆

What You Will Learn In This Chapter:

- ✓ The underlying issues behind sensory problems & their impact on a child
- ✓ Signs of underdevelopment for each sensory category
- ✓ Practical activities that promote better sensory integration for each sensory category

◆ ◆ ◆ ◆ ◆ ◆ ◆ ◆ ◆ ◆ ◆ ◆ ◆ ◆ ◆ ◆

One of the big ideas for this chapter is to understand that a sensory challenged child is an <u>*internally chaotic and insecure*</u> child, and thus externally and behaviorally chaotic. In this chapter, you will learn exactly why they are so chaotic and insecure and what you can do to help them. You will also come to a deeper understanding of the reasons behind my strategies – why we have to meet their internal needs and why is structure such an important piece for these children.

It's important to meet the child's internal sensory needs because the child is over or under stimulated in some of the sensory areas. Many challenging behaviors are a result of the child's inability to regulate sensory stimuli caused by sensory disintegration. Meeting the child's internal needs for sensory integration and structure <u>allows you to raise the bar on their external behavior and allows the child to achieve their full potential</u>.

While not all behaviors are rooted in unmet sensory needs, when a child's sensory needs are not met, it typically exhibits as poor behaviors. In this Chapter, I introduce you to the primary areas of sensory disintegration and what you can do to help your child meet his/her sensory needs.

For each area of sensory processing, I provide you

1. An explanation of what that sensory area entails and what role it plays in daily functions
2. Characteristics and symptoms of an underdeveloped sensory system in that area
3. An inventory list of activities your child can do to promote better sensory integration in that area

Use this chapter as a resource. Skim through the list of characteristics of the underdeveloped system to see which sensory area applies to your child. If your child exhibits some of the characteristics for a particular area, read on for more information on how to help your child. I recommend reading the proprioceptive area in its entirety because a very large majority of Children with SDN benefit from increased proprioceptive input. This is information based on my experience working with many Occupational Therapists and my own children over the years and these are the typical characteristics and the activities that promote better sensory integration. I recommend you consult with an Occupational Therapist to better understand your child's sensory system and then apply the associated strategies.

For best results, you want to tackle each deficient sensory area with a goal of keeping the "sensory cup" full.

Keep the "Sensory Cup" Full at All Times

Think of your child's sensory system as a cup that needs to be full at all times.

No one can realistically quantify for you the amount of input your child needs in each sensory area. But if sensory input is lacking, your child will start exhibiting symptoms and appear less calm and more anxious overall. This means their sensory cup may need a top-off, a refill, or possibly a dump if it is overfull. How do you fill the sensory cup? You fill the sensory cup by doing the sensory activities in the inventories I provide you below. The key is to start tuning yourself into your child's **"sensory cup"**, making sure that his/her sensory cup is full at all times. The cup is constantly draining due to the nature of a deficient system, so as the day goes on, the cup is getting lower and lower. Your job in providing the best support for your child is to gauge that cup and keep it full all the times. If at any time the cup is less than full or over full, the characteristics and symptoms will start showing up. If the cup is all the way empty, your life and your child's life can feel like a real misery - you probably know the feeling.

There are occupational therapists that put children on a "sensory diet", which is a schedule for when a child has to do certain sensory activities throughout the day. It could be every 30 minutes, every hour, every 2 hours, etc. that a child has to do a certain sensory activity. You could take that approach in order to ensure your child's sensory needs are met throughout the day; however, you won't really know what frequency and intensity your child needs unless you are gauging a child's **"sensory cup"**, as I suggested. So the best way is to gauge the sensory cup throughout the day and keep it full all day by leading your child into the provided list of proprioceptive activities. At times (especially for the auditory, visual, and tactile areas) it is also crucial to keep your child's cup from overflowing as a child with deficient sensory system cannot modulate the intake for themselves, causing system overload.

The material below on each of the sensory areas is presented in order of priority - what needs to be addressed first for best results in achieving sensory integration. First is the proprioceptive system, followed by vestibular, then auditory and so on.

Goals, Do's and Don'ts

Start off easy. Do not push the child into uncomfortable situations with sensory exposure or the child will build a defensive wall and resist more in the future.

If the child is under stimulated in a sensory area (such as proprioceptive, which is a common under stimulation area for many children), start off easy and increase gradually over time to achieve the right balance.

If a child is over stimulated in an area because the child doesn't have the threshold to tolerate the natural environmental stimuli, you want to start exposure very lightly and slowly as to not shock the system and not build more resistance to sensory stimuli.

When a child's threshold to stimuli is low, the child is easily over stimulated and under stress, which is why you want to increase the threshold over time, so the child will have a higher tolerance and won't be so easily over stimulated. For example, if your child typically melts down or has a behavior problem after x amount of auditory stimulation, after successfully raising the threshold, that meltdown will not happen anymore after x amount of visual stimuli because the threshold is raised and the child is more tolerant. That is your goal when it comes to over stimulation.

Your goal for under stimulation is to provide the right amount of stimulation so the child is no longer having sensory seeking behaviors to try to obtain the stimulation his/her system needs.

Thus, by addressing these internal needs first, you already will see a big improvement in behaviors. After sensory needs, you want to continue to the following chapters to learn how to address other internal needs. When the internal needs are addressed, you will be well positioned to tackle behaviors effectively, and you will also have less behaviors to tackle by then.

1. Proprioceptive (body awareness) System

Proprioception is the awareness of where one's body exists in space and coordination of body movements including direction and how much force to apply for different movements. Normally, this awareness is achieved by each joint firing up messages back to the brain about where the body part is, thus allowing the brain to draw an accurate conclusion of body awareness. When the neurons do not transmit that message back to the brain, or back to the right spot in the brain, it causes a proprioception problem. Proprioception problems can manifest into many behavioral areas that people may not consider related.

Proprioceptive system is the first system that needs to be addressed with most sensory children. The proprioceptive system helps the rest of the system function properly. A lack of proprioceptive input in the system will cause an existing auditory, visual, or tactile sensitivity to feel so much worse for the child (and for the adult). With a healthy proprioceptive system, a child will generally have more tolerance in the rest of the sensory areas even when they are deficient in other areas.

Usually, when proprioceptive is successfully addressed, caregivers should notice an improvement in behaviors related to the proprioceptive characteristics below.

Characteristics of Underdeveloped Proprioceptive System:

- Rambunctious in play, rough play, pushes kids on the playground, etc.
- Writes with too much pressure, breaking the lead of pencils, pressing too hard, or not hard enough to see the actual writing or coloring
- Physical hyperactivity or tiresome and sluggish
- Physically clumsy and uncoordinated, falling out of chairs, etc.
- Heavy footed (tends to stomp when walking, and have heavy movements)
- Lack of focus and concentration (and other ADHD-like symptoms), easily distracted
- Lack of impulse control
- Lack of self-regulation (agitated easily and struggles to calm himself)
- Frequent tantrums and meltdowns
- Fidget and unsettled

If your child exhibits the above symptoms, your child may hugely benefit from increased proprioceptive input, which consists of exercises with a joint compression nature. Joint compression is the key to increasing proprioception. You literally compress the joints of the body in order to fire that message back to the part of the brain that must receive it. This type of proprioceptive input helps increase body awareness, system orientation, and thus calms the child down in everyday life.

How Do I Start, How Much to Do It, How Do I Know it's Working?

Start with 10-15 minutes a day (cumulative) of any of the below proprioceptive input activities, and work up to 30 minutes a day. For some children, possibly up to an hour is required to keep the sensory cup full and, therefore, the system calm. You will find out how much your child needs - the gauge is improvement in the above symptoms. When the symptoms improve, you are on the right track.

Your job is to stay tuned in and find just the right level (quantity and intensity) of proprioceptive input your child needs each day in order to stay at optimum functioning and calmness. When the cup is full and the level is just right, you will notice things like improved concentration and focus, fewer tantrums (could be less in duration and/or intensity and/or frequency), less agitation, less walking on eggshells around your child, less hyperactivity, better self-control and impulse control - you will feel an overall sense of calmness from your child.

For the first 2-3 weeks, make no judgement or conclusion because like certain types of medication, an increase of proprioceptive input takes some time to get into and build up in the system. If your child has been lacking proprioceptive input for a while or all his/her life, it will take some time to "fill up" the cup. So give it a few weeks to build up and to fill up the sensory cup. Start small with the magnitude that is doable and comfortable for you and your child, and slowly work on building up to a higher quantity and intensity.

Proprioceptive Activity Inventory

A large majority of Children with SDN are experiencing proprioceptive under stimulation. The below activities increase proprioceptive input:

- **Bouncing & Jumping** - on trampoline, bed, from a couch to a pile of cushions, bouncing on bounce balls such as Hippity Hop ball
- **Running** - especially uphill and/or with weights
- **Going uphill or upstairs** - running or walking
- **Crawling** - bear crawl (on hands and feet, not knees)
- **Pushing** - push anything with weights: fill a box, wheelbarrow, wagon, or any push toy with weights (water jug, rocks, can food, beans, etc.) and push it around, find any heavy items to push around indoors or outdoors, anytime you can add uphill it increases the intensity
- **Pulling** – similar to the pushing, except have the child pull the heavy items
- **Shoveling** - dirt, sand, snow, etc.
- **Carrying weighted items** - loading/unloading groceries, weighted backpack, etc.
- **Weight training/resistance training** - if the child is old enough, any weight training or resistance training would serve as great proprioceptive input, either with free weights, weight machines, or stretchy bands

- **Swimming** - water provides resistance
- **Chewing crunchy hard items** - nuts, raw vegetables, and special oral chews, usually made of rubber. Chewing hard things increase proprioceptive input in the jaws

---

Anything that is considered a "resistance" workout is a great source of proprioceptive input. The general idea is to <u>embrace weight</u>. If you can keep a child's sensory cup full through the above proprioceptive input activities that will be the best. Don't forget the impact of endorphins produced during exercises which can be used as a natural mood stabilizer and mood enhancer.

When the proprioceptive sensory needs are too high

There are some children whose proprioceptive input need is so high that the child would practically have to be a cowboy or a farm boy working on a ranch or a farm from sunrise to sunset in order to meet the proprioceptive needs. For these children, such as my son, unless they really are farm boys/girls working outside all day, they really can't get their needs met being an urban school boy/girl sitting in classrooms most of the day. That's when tools like a weighted vest, weighted blankets, weighted straps, etc. come in. They are essentially weights that a child wears for either part of the day, or all day, depending on the needs, in order to compensate and provide additional proprioceptive input to the child's system. The most effective weighted vests are weighed **compression** vests, which not only provide proprioceptive input through weights, but also through compression – it squeezes all the joints of the child, providing direct joint compression.

In my personal opinion, the needs are preferably met through physical activities in the proprioceptive activity inventory, because there is no doubt that physical exercises provide endless benefits to a person's general health and wellbeing. But if your child is already doing 2-3 hours' worth of those activities every day and you just can't fit the 3rd or the 4th hour into your child's schedule due to school, etc., then go for the weighted vest to help you reach the rest of your child's proprioceptive "quota", while keeping the same level of physical activities.

When first starting a weighted vest, start off with low weight (5-10% of child's body weight) as to not overwhelm the system, and again, gauge your child's sensory cup over the course of several days or 1-2 weeks to decide if that is a good weight. My analogy here is working the medication dosage for a child - you are constantly giving feedback to your psychiatrist to find just the right dose. If your child is wearing a weighted vest with too much weight, your child will start getting sleepy and shutting down. If the weight is too low, your child will continue to exhibit the above symptoms of proprioceptive deficiency. A general guideline for weights in weighted vest is 10% of body weight, but this number is very personal depending on the child, the activity level, and where the child is with his/her overall sensory needs.

Final notes on proprioceptive input

Do the activities in the inventory. They will make a big difference in your child's ability to function in his/her day-to-day life, not to mention the added benefits of exercise in general. Endorphins produced from exercise serve as a natural mood enhancer that also benefits the child with SDN. It will also take the edge off on all those tantrums and meltdowns. The most important thing is to keep it fun and keep it varied. At some point, a couple of my children needed more than 2 hours of these activities per day to get their sensory cups to 70% full (which isn't full), and doing all those exercises for that much time every day was beginning to bore them. You don't want your child to be bored with it. You want to keep it fun and keep it fresh. It cannot become a punishment for being hyper and acting wild, for example. Although, if your child is being hyper and acting wild, clearly some proprioceptive activities are due/overdue. The key is to keep it fun and varied so it is a sustainable lifestyle. Many times I do these activities with my children to give me some exercises and make it fun for them that we're doing it together.

Also remember, if you filled their cup from 5% to 20% full, their cup is still very far from being full. In that case, it doesn't matter that you just had your child bouncing on the trampoline 5 minutes ago for 20 minutes, the cup is still quite empty. It will take some time to fill it up in this case....

2. Vestibular (movement) System

The vestibular system is located in the inner ear. It is in charge of movements and balance. The fluid in the inner ear moves as we tilt and move our heads, and it gives the body information about spatial awareness, which provides balance and a sense of gravity so we won't fall. The vestibular system also assists with effective eye movement and auditory processing.

An underdeveloped vestibular system causes struggles in our interactions with surroundings, which contribute to part of the meltdown and what appears to be a fragile emotional state.

Characteristics of underdeveloped Vestibular System:

- Overly sensitive to movements - feeling unbalanced and insecure or afraid during movements
- Under responsive to movements - appears to need to move constantly, sometimes this can look like physical hyper activeness
- Clumsy, uncoordinated movements - running into things, tripping and falling
- Poor posture - have a hard time sitting, standing, or walking upright, leaning body on furniture and walls, doesn't stand up straight or sit up straight
- Motor planning difficulties - trouble skipping, catching balls, seems to lack agility in sports. This motor planning difficulty can also include oral motor difficulties and mouth movement coordination, which may cause speech problems
- Coordination of movement also can result in difficulties with visual tracking activities like reading or copying something off the whiteboard

If your child exhibits the above characteristics, use the below inventory to promote a more developed vestibular system.

Vestibular Activity Inventory
- **Swinging** - swinging side to side, front to back, circular, fast or slow, high or low. This is why we swing or rock our babies to sleep - this vestibular input is soothing and calming
- **Running** - running provides vestibular input and motion, running with weights or uphill can provide both vestibular and proprioceptive input
- **Rocking** – any movements that involve a rocking motion
- **Playing on the playground** - hanging upside down on monkey bars
- **Playing on the slides** - fast movement
- **Spinning** - on an office chair or stool, spinning toys, merry go round
- **Somersaults**
- **Balancing** - walk on beam, walk across a cushion or bed while maintaining balance, walk on the curb, etc.
- **Jumping & bouncing** - trampoline provides both proprioceptive and vestibular input, jump rope, jumping jacks

While vestibular input creates a soothing and calming effect for children (and adults), the combination of too much vestibular activity such as swinging, and not enough proprioceptive input will actually have the opposite effect of causing a child to turn giggly, silly and out of control. If this happens, immediately facilitate proprioceptive activities to calm the system back down.

3. Tactile System

Our tactile system processes the information we get from our skin receptors, helping the system interpret how we feel when something touches our skin. The information processed by the tactile system includes texture, pressure, temperature, etc., and helps us decide if the water is too hot or just right; if clothing feels too rough or just right on our skin. It is the sensory system that tells you to withdraw your hand if you accidentally touched the hot stovetop, and it is there to protect you from danger. A well-functioning tactile system filters out which tactile input is important and unimportant. It helps a child feel comfortable and not distracted by clothing and socks on the skin, or even the way the breeze and air feels on their face, and any other tactile stimuli. On the other hand, a child with an immature tactile system will have a hard time going along with many of the daily events that don't usually bother others.

Characteristics of underdeveloped tactile System:

- Struggles with daily hygiene tasks - bathing, shampooing the hair, haircutting, tooth brushing, etc. May experience crying and tantrums during these tasks

- Difficulties with certain clothing - shirts, socks, etc. never feels right for the child
- Seeking out for tactile input - touching everything they see; putting their hand out to swipe through all the cars in the parking lot as he/she walks by, for example
- Always touching and playing with objects - their own clothing, zipper, hair...
- Tendency to be physically close to others to seek tactile input - touching, hugging, sitting very closely

Some of these behaviors are sensory seeking, wanting to find more tactile input, while some are sensory avoiding, not wanting to have the tactile input on their skin. Exposure to various sensory items will help desensitize and/or obtain the child's desired input. If your child is sensitive to tactile input, start slow as to not overwhelm the child.

Tactile Activity Inventory

For the tactile hypersensitive child, on the one hand, you need to minimize stimulation in order for them to get along with themselves and the clothing on their skin; on the other hand, you need to slowly increase the tactile exposure in order to build up their threshold so that they can eventually tolerate the various daily tactile stimuli.

- Start with **easier tactile exposure** - playing with tub of beans, rice, pasta, sand, etc. Scooping,

pouring, dumping with utensils, then hands to get more tactile input
- Move onto **further tactile exposure** - dough, slime, finger paint, clay, etc.
- Finally move on to the **harder to tolerate inputs** – such as shaving cream or any slimy sticky textures that sticks to the hands and doesn't come off easily
- **Play in messy things** - mud, dirt, or sand
- **Play with squishy fidgeting toys** - squeeze balls, stretchy rubber toys
- **Explore texture in bath** - with different types of soap, loofa, and sponges in bath to build tolerance through fun playing/bathing/experimenting. Do only as much as the child can tolerate and build up from there, each time trying something new
- **Selective clothing** - until threshold is built up, go through the closet and have the child pull out any clothing or socks and hats that they dislike (usually because they don't feel right on their skin from the tactile perspective). Until they build up a more developed tactile system, avoid those items for a while to reduce meltdowns
- **Sensory friendly clothing** - If needed, after pulling out clothing that doesn't feel good, purchase a few pieces of sensory friendly clothing such as seamless socks or extremely soft undergarment

4. Auditory System

The inner organs of our ears not only hear sounds, but also interprets sounds. What is the sound? Is it soothing or alarming? What action do I need to take? A normally functioning auditory system is not only able to hear the sound of a parent calling and interpret what it means, but is also able to send a signal to the brain and body to take appropriate actions, such as acting upon a parent's request or responding to a parent's call. It is also able to filter out the unimportant information while processing and acting upon the important information. A compromised auditory system does not function as above, causing difficulties in a child's daily functions, and further disorganization and insecurity about one's environment.

Characteristics of Underdeveloped Auditory System:

- Unable to function with a noisy surrounding - may meltdown or simply be distracted from the task at hand and become unable to perform tasks
- Overwhelmed or startled by unpredictable common sounds in the environment
- Poor listening skills, communication skills, and social skills
- Misinterpret information he/she hears, or miss subtle information and words
- Withdrawn from a noisy and crowded environment
- Agitated and in distress often, especially in noisy environments
- Slow to respond to verbal cues such as calling of his/her name or verbal instructions

- Difficulties responding to and remembering verbal instructions
- Appearing to be making noise all the time - singing, humming, talking, in attempt to give himself more auditory input
- Appears to not hear you at times

Auditory Activity Inventory

- **Direction following & listening activities** - "Simon says", etc.
- **Provide visual charts** - it helps a child with auditory processing difficulties to have another way to receiving information. This is a compensation not an activity to improve auditory processing. See later chapters to learn about visual charts.
- **Movement songs** - hand movements or finger movements connecting movements with sounds
- **Provide additional auditory input** - playing with instruments, listening to music, clapping and making sounds with their own body, headphones, sound machines

Specific strategies to help an auditory hypoactive child concentrate in this work or not get overwhelmed:

- **Provide a quiet space** to retreat to when overwhelmed with sounds and noises

- **Provide earplugs or noise canceling headsets** for noisy environments to protect from overwhelm while working on building threshold for noise

---

5. Visual System

The visual system not only sees, but also interprets and communicates with the brain what we see and what actions to take. For example, if we see a hairy leg bug, most people have goose bumps as an action the body takes based on the visual input. The intricacies of visual processing includes visual discrimination, visual memory (remembering what you see), visual motor abilities, visual form, visual scanning, etc. A child with visual processing problems cannot interact with his/her surroundings effectively.

Characteristics of an Underdeveloped Visual System:

- Distracted or overwhelmed by visual stimuli - colorful and busy walls, posters, busy patterns on furniture or backgrounds, flooring, activities outside the window, etc.
- Inability to focus on tasks at hand due to visual distraction
- Has trouble finding things in his environment - doesn't see what he is looking for even if it's right in front of him.
- Trouble with visual activities - puzzles, I spy books, matching games, etc.

Visual Input Activity Inventory
To help a visually hyperactive child:

- ***Provide clean, neat, and visually simple environments for work*** space - minimize posters, wall hangings, provide consistent color in the room, no bright lighting
- ***Further minimize distraction*** - work on a desk facing a blank wall or use a cardboard divider to block visual distractions
- ***Reading help*** - use a blank paper to keep track of the line the child is reading, moving the blank paper down as the child finishes reading each line

To help a visually hypoactive child:

- ***Provide additional visual stimuli*** - provide learning materials in bright and colorful fashion

6. Oral Sensory System

We perceive texture, taste, and temperature through the receptors in our mouths. We also generate our speech through these oral receptors inside our mouth. Children with well-developed oral sensory systems typically have a varied diet and are willing to try a variety of food and do not put inappropriate objects into their mouth to seek oral sensory input.

Characteristics of underdeveloped Oral Sensory System:

- Struggles to brush teeth and visit the dentist, resulting in tantrums and meltdowns
- Has a limited diet - unwilling to try new foods, will only eat and tolerate a fixed set of foods, such as familiar choices with certain textures
- Gagging or choking with certain foods
- Uncomfortable using utensils to eat - uncomfortable with the texture and touch of utensils inside their mouth
- Puts inappropriate objects in the mouth to gain oral sensory stimuli - clothing, fingers, hands, toys, pens/pencils, anything they can find.
- Stuff too much food in the mouth at once
- Make noise with their mouth - humming, clicking tongue, etc.
- Poor articulation (sound production) in speech

If your child is struggling a lot with mealtime and feeding, consider visiting a specialized feeding clinic or an occupational therapist.

Oral Sensory Activity Inventory

- ***Provide chew toys to increase oral sensory input*** in order to help manage behaviors, or to increase exposure and build a wider threshold
- ***Use a vibrating toothbrush*** or put vibrating toys on the cheek to increase oral stimuli

- *Chewing crunchy foods* - nuts, raw carrots, crunchy chips, etc.
- *Experimenting with a variety of texture and taste in foods* - hard, soft, mushy, crunchy, chewy, slippery, smooth, rough, carbonated water; sweet, sour, salty,
- *Blowing bubbles*, whistles, recorders, balloons

Again, start off slowly with variety experimentation. First set the new food in their plate. As they tolerate the new food in their plate, encourage them to touch and play with the food. As they can tolerate touching the food, move onto taking a small bite, then chewing, maybe another bite. Go slow. Make it fun.

7. The Olfactory System (smell)

Our olfactory system not only controls our sense of smell, but is also associated with our limbic system, which controls memory and emotions in the nervous system.

Characteristics of underdeveloped Olfactory System:

- Overly sensitive to smells that normally don't bother others - can gag or get agitated
- Overly drawn to smells - hold objects like crayons, markers, etc. close to the nose to smell them

Olfactory Activity Inventory

- ***Experiment with smells*** through cooking together
- ***Play with scented objects*** - scented stickers, markers, bubbles
- ***Combine tactile and olfactory activity*** by adding essential oils (lavender, peppermint, lemon, etc.) to tubs of beans, rice, pasta, etc. to add a scent to the tactile play
- ***Experiment with a variety of essential oils*** added to playdough

Departing thoughts on sensory needs

After skimming through the activity inventories for each of the sensory areas. Do you notice something? Most of these activities will be achieved by simply taking the child to the playground and spending time out in nature, especially the proprioceptive and vestibular areas - climbing, running around and playing on the playground; the tactile input from touching and exploring all kinds of things in nature, sand, dirt, rocks, auditory input through hearing birds, olfactory stimulation exposure from smelling a variety of flowers, etc.

It has become clear to me that part of the reason that sensory problems are becoming such an epidemic nowadays is due to the advancement in technologies, urbanization and such, which compromise a lot of time that a child would have otherwise spent outside. Think of your own childhood or your parents/grandparents childhood stories, what did they do all day? Playing on the street, running around the fields, in the mountains, working outside till dusk? Back in those days, say my grandparents' days (or even my parents'), they didn't use fancy words like "proprioceptive" and "vestibular", and didn't have parents, teachers and caregivers like you who are seeking and reaching out to learn more about how to get the sensory needs met. How did our parents and grandparents ever get their sensory needs met without all this information? Simple, they spent much of their time outside and they got far more input than a child on a sensory diet.

My point is, in a more urbanized environment with more advanced technologies, where children are sitting in class all day and spending a lot of time in front of a screen, as opposed to working or playing on a farm, ranch, or field all day, we (parents, teachers, caregivers) have to be far more intentional about creating movements and outdoor opportunities to meet the sensory needs of our children. Look at the benefits of going outside that directly help us with the struggles we are dealing with in our children's mood, behaviors, and day-to-day functions: proprioceptive, vestibular, and a wide variety of sensory input; vitamin D absorbed through sun exposure which helps with mood; endorphins generated through physical activities which is a natural mood enhancer; fresh air…. list goes on. Our family goes on hikes almost every weekend and frequently have daily walks around the neighborhood. It's part of the lifestyle we love and it happens to support our Children with SDN, promoting better mood, self-regulation, sensory input, and a lot more.

After all the fancy terms and strategies, I want to leave you and this chapter with a departing thought - Get back to simple and go play outside.

I hope this chapter has laid a foundation for you on why the strategies from the following chapters on structure, etc. are so crucial. Due to the sensory difficulties, the child is generally less able to interpret sensory information and respond appropriately, and this disorientation within themselves with respect to their surrounding is a big source of their internal distress, chaos, and insecurity. Because of this disorientation with their surroundings, and the insecurity that comes with it, the Children with SDN have divergent needs and require additional concrete support in many areas. These additional concrete strategies are introduced in the following chapters.

♦ ♦ ♦ ♦ ♦ ♦ ♦ ♦ ♦ ♦ ♦ ♦ ♦ ♦ ♦ ♦

Your Take-Away From This Chapter:

- ✓ Keep the "sensory cup" full at all times
- ✓ Create opportunities for movements and outdoor play
- ✓ Get the big picture - Sensory disintegration causes a lot of internal chaos and insecurity in a child, thus the child needs more structure and additional support to function optimally

♦ ♦ ♦ ♦ ♦ ♦ ♦ ♦ ♦ ♦ ♦ ♦ ♦ ♦ ♦ ♦

CHAPTER 8
The Framework That Deflates Your Child's Anxiety

♦ ♦ ♦ ♦ ♦ ♦ ♦ ♦ ♦ ♦ ♦ ♦ ♦ ♦ ♦

What You Will Learn In This Chapter:

- ✓ Why structure is so important for the child with Sensitive Divergent Needs
- ✓ How to create structure in a child's life

♦ ♦ ♦ ♦ ♦ ♦ ♦ ♦ ♦ ♦ ♦ ♦ ♦ ♦ ♦

In the past, I have had numerous frustrated parents (especially stay-at-home parents who have their children all day) come to me asking for advice on how to get their child under control. Their general complaint is that the child is "all over the place, running through the house getting into trouble, not coming when I call him to eat, not going to sleep when he needs to, etc."

My first question is, "Do you have a regular consistent schedule and routine for your child such that he knows exactly what he is supposed to do and when?" The answer is usually: "No, we just hang out all day, sometimes go to the park, sometimes go to the store, play at home, etc." You may know when your child is supposed to eat, go to the park, play by himself at home, do homework, go to sleep and what not, but your child may not, or at least not to the clarity of internal and external self-organization. Hence the "all over the place" feeling of chaos.

My very first advice – Build structure into your child's life.

Why is structure so important?
All children need a certain degree of structure in their environment for them to do well, some more, some less. Children with SDN tend to have a much higher need for structure than others due to the previously explained lack of orientation with respect to the environment (sensory induced) and thus a lack of security. Recalling our wild drive to the grocery store analogy from a previous chapter, when you are unable to receive and process incoming information, you feel disoriented, unsafe, insecure, and thus you have a higher need for security - things that are predictable to you to help you navigate through this wild drive. By "structure", I mean knowing the where, when, and what of my day (or of a segment of time).

In our wild drive to the grocery store analogy, wouldn't you feel a little more grounded and secure if you at least knew that there are no random rocks on the road that you can bump into, and there are absolutely no turns or ice on the road for another mile, or one mile where you can just go straight without worrying about lane changes and making turns of stopping under those terrible conditions? That's called predictability. Your child with SDN needs predictability for the same reason you would need it in that hypothetical wild drive to the grocery store.

Most adults have a planner of some sort, it could be daily, weekly, or monthly and some have all of the above. As an adult, most of you wake up in the morning and need to know what your plans are today (appointments, scheduled events, things to do, things to get done, etc.), even if the plan was just as vague as "go to work, come home, walk my dog, have dinner, meet Terry for coffee and go to sleep." The point is, at any moment in time, *you have an idea of what you're doing* for the next 5 minutes, 1 hour, or half the day and so on.

Children in general need structure to feel secure and to strive. That's why schools have various periods and snack time, lunch time, recess time, etc. In preschools, just within a couple of hours, children have structure – circle time, potty time, center time, story time, art time, wait for pick-up time, etc. Generally speaking, the younger the children, the more structure they require. Likewise, the higher the needs, the more structure they require as well. Some special needs children need a schedule for 10 minutes worth of time – they have a need to know what the next 10 minutes of their time is going to look like; where will they be, what they will do, and when will they be done. Those are the questions that many children cannot answer for themselves unless their plans are communicated to them, so that they actually have a sense of time.

Some children with divergent needs have special needs that cause them to not have a sense of how much time has passed. When you have jet lag, you finish your meal with your body thinking it's time to go to sleep for the night when it is actually morning time. Children with certain special needs feel that way all the time because their brains can't tell time the way an average person can. And most young children are this way anyway due to the nature of immature development at that age. When they don't know what they are doing, when they are doing it, and when they will be done, they feel insecure and very chaotic internally. Wouldn't you too if you lost your schedule book, planner, or whatever you use to conduct your day, and on top of that you lost your watch too (phone, or whatever you use to tell time)? Young children don't know how to read the clock. That internal feeling of chaos in a child with SDN can quickly turn into external chaos and eventually escalate into behavior problems or an emotional melt-down. Thus it is important to create and introduce structure (schedules and routines) into their lives to help them organize themselves internally and therefore organize themselves externally in any environment.

How to create and introduce structure into their lives

For any given time, your child with SDN would feel far more secure and organized if he had a visual display of what's going to happen – what am I doing, when am I doing it, where, and when will I be done.

Consistent routines

For everyday life, it is important to have consistent routines. A routine could be as high level and vague as "weekdays we go to school, weekends we go hiking and swimming", or it could be as detailed and refined as "bedtime routine – brush teeth → put jammies on → read a story → shut lights → sleep". Depending on your child's specific needs, you need to create consistent routines at as many levels as your child needs– weekly, daily, hour segments, few minute segments, etc. The more chaotic and inharmonious your child seems, the more structure and details he may need, especially in new situations. It needs to be predictable to them. They need to have a general awareness of what happens when. Knowing what happens when and having this sense of predictability enhances their sense of security and thus enhances their ability to cope with stress. Remember, they are under constant stress with their surroundings due to sensory issues.

Below are some examples of structured routines, making things more predictable for the child with SDN. Once you create a routine, try to keep it consistent so it's predictable. See figures 8-1, 8-2, 8-3.

Weekly Schedule Example

	Monday	Tuesday	Wednesday	Thursday	Friday	Saturday	Sunday
Daytime	School	School	School	School	School	Hiking	Church
Night time	Soccer	Home	Home	Swimming	Movie Night	Cook Together	Relax & Play

Knowing what always happens on what day of the week is predictability, which increases security

© 2017 Harmonious Clan

Figure 8- 1 Weekly Schedule Example

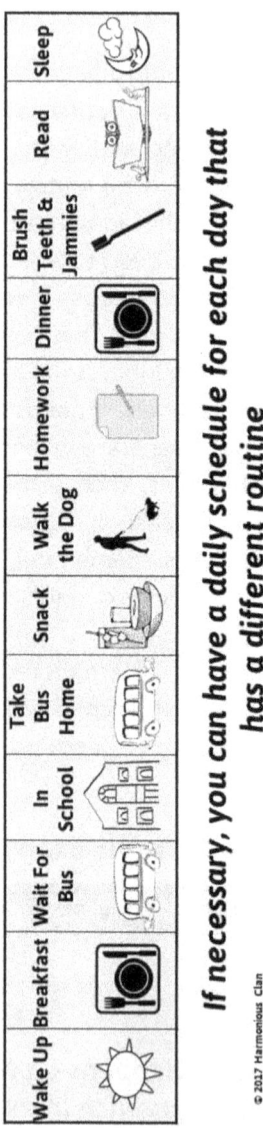

Figure 8-2 Daily Schedule Example

A Small Segment of Daily Time Schedule Example

Bedtime Schedule

Figure 8-3 Example Bedtime Schedule

They need to see it

For most children, mentally knowing what they are doing, when they are doing it and where isn't effective enough when they don't have ready access to that information. They need something to look at, something concrete for reference. They need a visual representation of the schedule or plan. This is when pictorial visual charts become very useful in helping them <u>see, or visualize</u> their schedule, part of their world. See more about visual charts in the next chapter.

◆ ◆ ◆ ◆ ◆ ◆ ◆ ◆ ◆ ◆ ◆ ◆ ◆ ◆ ◆

Your Take-Away From This Chapter:

✓ Structure provides predictability, which provides security for the child with Sensitive Divergent Needs

◆ ◆ ◆ ◆ ◆ ◆ ◆ ◆ ◆ ◆ ◆ ◆ ◆ ◆ ◆

CHAPTER 9
The Simple Amazing Tool That Boosts Your Child's Cooperation

♦ ♦ ♦ ♦ ♦ ♦ ♦ ♦ ♦ ♦ ♦ ♦ ♦ ♦ ♦ ♦ ♦

What You Will Learn In This Chapter:

- ✓ Why visual charts are important for the child with Sensitive Divergent Needs
- ✓ How to incorporate visual chart into various daily uses

♦ ♦ ♦ ♦ ♦ ♦ ♦ ♦ ♦ ♦ ♦ ♦ ♦ ♦ ♦ ♦ ♦

Visual charts are an important part of helping your child to manage his daily life and to keep things in order for him. Visual charts help provide a clear and vivid vision of whatever message you are trying to convey to your audience. Why is it important to have visual charts for your child?

"A picture says a thousand words." This is true even for older children who can already read very well. Imagine reading this book if I took out all of the diagrams, figures and drawings. Certain ideas are much more easily conveyed and received in a visual form. Your visual charts don't actually have to be pictures; it just needs to be a place to visually see things. It could be simple written words, but the fewer the words the better.

Having visual aids minimizes the amount of information your child must process, therefore creating a much more straight forward way to communicate ideas with your child, and for your child to keep himself organized independently. There are several areas where you can employ visual charts:

Schedule and Daily Routines

As explained in the previous chapter, it is important to provide external structure to help your child manage his internal chaos. As you structure your child's day for him, your structure isn't really structure for him until he can clearly see it and interpret it. This is largely true for adults too. For example, what percentage of busy adults prefer to manage their day without a daily calendar or planner of some sort, be it paper or electronic device? Not many. Most busy adults feel lost without their daily planner to check their appointments and commitments. Most adults need a visual aid for their schedule (there are apps for that), and your child with SDN especially needs the visual aids to help him interpret and process the schedule. He needs to see it to know what he is doing now, what he is doing next and so forth.

You may say that they know their schedule in their head, however, actually putting it down on paper either in a drawing or single words creates a whole other layer of structure, security, and certainty for them. To see it feels so much more concrete than to know it in their heads, especially for the profile children we are discussing in this book. Please refer to the previous chapter for samples of schedule and routine visual charts.

Transition charts

In chapter 10 (The 7 Effective Techniques That Achieve Successful Transitions), you will learn 7 powerful transition strategies. While you employ the transition strategies discussed in chapter 10, it is helpful to have a transition chart for your child to visually see exactly what to expect before, during, and after the transition. Transitions have every reason to be hard for our children, and you will learn why in chapter 10. It is especially helpful to include in your visual aid whatever behaviors you are expecting from your child during this transition.

For example, I created a chart for my son (Figure 9-1) who has the hardest time during transitions. Since a very young age, my son blew every transition there is to blow, including the ones that don't even count as a transition for most people. Simple tasks such as remaining at the same table and seat while he finishes one craft and begins another craft are a major transition to him. What seems like a simple task to move on to the next craft for most people can cause a blow up for him even when I am the one moving him on to the next craft. He would throw things, yell, cry, and kick during these minimal transitions. I created a chart for him that outlined the behavioral expectations during transition time: hands and feet to myself, soft voice, calm, and stay in control, etc. Every time before the transition I would show him his transition chart, review it with him, discuss it, rehearse it with him, then we would have the transition. It was very effective in much more smoothly managing his transitions.

Transition Chart

© 2017 Harmonious Clan

Figure 9- 1 Example Transition Chart

Choice Charts

When offering choices, it is helpful to have choice charts handy for the routine options your child has. Having a visual choice chart helps your child organize his thoughts during his evaluation of his choices, and visually emphasizes to your child the fact that he has choices, which is a positive thing. Items for which I have personally created visual choice charts include

- Our token reward system menu - a visual chart of all the good things the child gets to choose as a reward for good behaviors
- Break activity choice - things a child can choose to do for fun when he takes a break after finishing a task or work

- Down time choice chart - things a child can choose from to do during unstructured down times
- Exercise choice chart - helps a child decide what exercise he would like to do when it's time to exercise
- and a lot more

Choice charts help give your child options, help your child learn the process of decision making, and provides some structure to your child's process. For example, when it's down time, what can I do? If the choices and options aren't readily available and visually accessible, there is a much higher chance of this child resorting to troublesome behaviors as default time killers. Choice charts help him structure his thinking and his process. Below (Figure 9-2) is an example of a choice chart for down time.

Figure 9- 2 Example Choice Chart - Down Time

Responsibilities, Chores, and Work Charts

Whenever you need your child to understand and meet a requirement, be it a chore, homework, any responsibility or task, the execution of the task can go more smoothly when the exact tasks or steps are visually displayed.

For example, we have after-dinner clean up chores for all the children where every child helps clean the big dinner production by doing their portion of the cleanup job. This dinner cleanup also leads to some of the evening bedtime routines. Our three year old son at the time had the responsibility of bringing his own dishes back to the kitchen and sweeping the dining room floor; next he had to brush teeth and put on his jammies. In order for him to keep himself accountable for all of his responsibilities, I created a job chart for him (Figure 9-3):

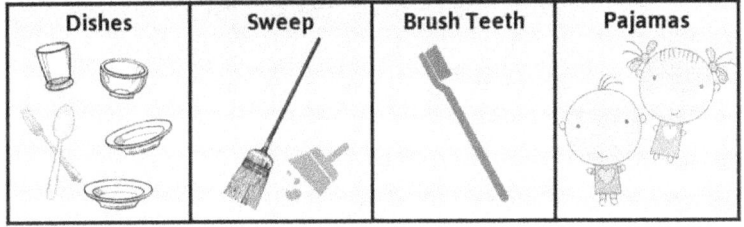

Figure 9- 3 Example Job Chart

He would do each job, check if off his chart, find out what is his next job, do it and check it off until everything on his chart was checked off.

Expectation charts

My transition chart outlining expected behaviors during transitions also fits as an example of an expectation chart. Whatever expectations you have for your child during certain situations, display those expectations for him visually and rehearse it. It helps so much as a reminder tool and an agreement between you and the child of what he is expected to do. I have an expectation chart for our family dinner that outlines the expected behaviors at the dining table.

◆ ◆ ◆ ◆ ◆ ◆ ◆ ◆ ◆ ◆ ◆ ◆ ◆ ◆ ◆ ◆

Your Take-Away From This Chapter:

- ✓ Visual charts help make things more concrete, tangible, and easier for the child with Sensitive Divergent Needs

◆ ◆ ◆ ◆ ◆ ◆ ◆ ◆ ◆ ◆ ◆ ◆ ◆ ◆ ◆ ◆

CHAPTER 10
The 7 Effective Techniques That Achieve Successful Transitions

♦ ♦ ♦ ♦ ♦ ♦ ♦ ♦ ♦ ♦ ♦ ♦ ♦ ♦ ♦

What You Will Learn In This Chapter:

✓ 7 Strategies to help your child transition more smoothly

♦ ♦ ♦ ♦ ♦ ♦ ♦ ♦ ♦ ♦ ♦ ♦ ♦ ♦ ♦

Transitions are especially difficult for many Children with SDN. Given their sensory issues (as you learned in Chapter 3), Children with SDN find it very difficult to face changes or transitions. Think about it, the child doesn't know where his body is (proprioceptive deficit), doesn't have a good handle on many of the natural environmental stimuli, and he finally just figured out what's going on around him and how to handle himself. Then suddenly, there is a change. To the child the idea of a change is frightening and stressful. If you still remember your wild drive to the grocery store analogy in Chapter 3, what if you suddenly find out a road closure and the need for a detour to somewhere you don't even know? Wouldn't that make things worse for you? Since a large part of our work in helping your child with SDN be successful is in meeting his needs, I dedicate this chapter on meeting his needs through transition times with specific transition strategies. Your child needs your support to help him transition smoothly. Below are specific strategies you can employ to help your child transition more smoothly:

1. Advanced notice leading to count-down

Advanced notice of the transitions and events that are coming is absolutely necessary. Just as you wouldn't like to be called into a work meeting at the last minute, your child wouldn't want to be asked to change what he is doing at the last minute. To better support your child through the transitions, tell the child what is about to come and what to expect ahead of time. The simplest example is when our children are all playing happily and they need to clean up and move to the dinner table. I would give them an advance notice by letting them know that play time is ending in 10 minutes and they need to clean up and come to dinner. I remind them again 5 minutes later, and again 2 minutes before clean up time. They are far more likely to transition out of a very pleasurable activity into a less-fun activity gracefully when they have advance notice.

2. Rehearse and priming

Continuing with my above example of from-cleaning-to-dinner example, I'd also rehearse with them what happens when

I call "playtime is over, come to dinner". We walk through this together – first we stop what we are doing, then we work together to clean (no fighting, no arguing about who cleans what), everything goes back to its place and we calmly walk to the dining table and quiety sit down. You need to vividly walk through the specific steps of the transition and prepare them as best as you can prior to the event. Depending on the level of difficulty for a certain transition, I may rehearse and prime in details one or two times in between my 1-3 advanced notices.

Rehearse the transition with your child and provide a step by step outline of your expectations. Rehearse it until he knows what he is to do and what you expect from him. He will be much more likely to transition smoothly because, through the rehearsing, he has already been through it.

3. Practice

Certain transitions need practice. For example, when my son was having a very difficult time getting out of the house because he had so much anxiety around transitions and changes, I used to piece out the events. For example, putting socks and shoes on. We would practice that event alone during the day when we were not actually going anywhere. The practice occurred at a leisure time as opposed to the chaotic and anxious time of a real transition and this practice helped when we came to an actual transition time that was filled with anxiety (even if it's excitement) and moving parts.

Practice those difficult transitions with your child at a time when he is not anxious about a real transition. Leisurely go through the process with your child several times before the actual transition.

The practice at a non-anxious time makes the child see that he can not only make transition, but can do so smoothly.

4. Visual aids

There are two types of visual aids you could use to help:

1) New situations - Pictures that give them an idea of what this transition or the **new situation** may look like before it actually happens. My personal examples of this are reviewing pictures of the new house to our son (2 years old at the time) weeks prior to our cross-country move and showing pictures of his important belongings and how they will be in our new house too when we get there; showing our son detailed pictures of the school that he was about to attend. (He never ended up really attending any schools for various reasons but lots of detailed class pictures were part of the preparation). Those were major life events to a child, but even for daily events like going to the grocery store or library, if you can talk through a mental picture of the grocery store or library, it helps them feel more secure and it helps them mentally put themselves in that environment before they have to physically transition there. The mental picture of the transition helps make the transition easier for them.

    The next time you are facing a new situation with your child, prepare your child with pictures. The pictures and mental images will ease the anxiety of the new situation and make it go more smoothly for all involved.

2) Transition Process - Pictures/drawings that show them what the **transition process** looks like. For example, when my son was young, before we went to the store, I used to pull up a chart that diagramed for my son the process of our transition (Figure 10-1):

Visual Chart Example

| Use Restroom | Get Socks & Shoes On | Get in Car | Buckle Up |

© 2017 Harmonious Clan

Figure 10- 1 Visual Chart Example

This helps the child visualize the specific steps that go into this transition process. All these visual aids are meant to help the child transition with a vivid image of certainty, because there are a lot of uncertainties. You are trying to stabilize the knowns to him. Some of these examples were done for young toddlers and preschoolers, but I still do something similar for a 7 year old especially for difficult transitions - even though he knows much better. It still helps his mental process in preparing himself for the new situation, just as it helps an adult athlete visualize scoring when he vividly visualizes himself putting that ball into the hoop.

Make some transitional charts or drawings for your child's difficult transitions. It doesn't have to be a major art project. A basic sketch or outline of the transition will suffice. You will be amazed at how the visual drawing can ease the transition for your child.

5. Transitional Object

My son used to always want to take a hat, a toy, or something important with him every time we were going somewhere. He always picked an object that was very important to him. I always fought to have him leave those objects at home so he wouldn't lose them because if he lost them he'd have a tough meltdown and a very hard time recovering from the loss. It was always a very difficult fight to have him leave his important objects at home until I realized why he absolutely "needed" to bring them with him. Once I realized the importance to him of the transitional object, I never fought him again. The reason it is important for him to bring a certain object with him is because it serves as his "transitional object", which provides him a sense of security. When things are changing and he doesn't know what's to come, where he is going, what things are going to be like for him, in the midst of all this chaos he must grab onto something that is more tangible and something that doesn't change so he can feel that "even though everything is changing, my hat is still going to be the same and it's still going to be with me." It is important to let your child use a transitional object if it is a stabilizing and calming object for him. After all, it is a coping mechanism to have something stable during changes and unknowns, wouldn't you do the same if put in that situation?

6. Managing Themselves During Transitions and Brief Idle Times During Transitions

Since we have five children, transitions can easily look like the zoo if not managed properly. Adding a few Children with SDN in the mix, it can be even worse than a zoo. Children often don't know what to do with themselves and start putting their hands and feet on others, bothering others, being disruptive. A trick is to display pictures of what-can-I-do options for them during transitions. Many of these options consist of sensory activities such as squeezing their hands and body parts tightly and then releasing to relax those parts; push-ups, if appropriate; breathing exercises; being in a certain yoga pose; reading a book, etc. It's something to keep them busy and out of trouble. The visual display of these options is very helpful to them. Even when I was waiting at a grocery checkout line with my son, he learned self-management skills.

Create charts and visual aids with options for your child during idle times. The charts provide them with options so they have a choice of what to do, the difference is that all the choices are the proper behaviors they need to learn for self-management.

7. Something to Look Forward To

Transitions are difficult, so it helps to have something to look forward to. For example, back to my previous example of transitioning from playing to cleaning and dining, it helps if the child knows that even though he has to stop doing the fun thing he's doing (playing) and do something he doesn't enjoy doing (cleaning), when he's done he has something to look forward to (e.g. his favorite meal waiting at the table).

For each difficult transition your child faces, pick a couple or even a few of these transition strategies to implement. Your child's transition and, therefore, yours will go more smoothly. The idea is that transitions are difficult for children, so what can you do to help make it easier? Any of the above strategies help tackle this problem. Play with it and see what fits your child's style, then stick what works.

◆ ◆ ◆ ◆ ◆ ◆ ◆ ◆ ◆ ◆ ◆ ◆ ◆ ◆ ◆ ◆ ◆

Your Take-Away From This Chapter:

- ✓ Transitions are especially hard for children with SDN
- ✓ Support your child's transitions with one or more of these 7 transition strategies

◆ ◆ ◆ ◆ ◆ ◆ ◆ ◆ ◆ ◆ ◆ ◆ ◆ ◆ ◆ ◆ ◆

CHAPTER 11
The Powerful, Easy to Implement Process That Simplifies the Teaching of New Behaviors

◆ ◆ ◆ ◆ ◆ ◆ ◆ ◆ ◆ ◆ ◆ ◆ ◆ ◆ ◆ ◆ ◆

What You Will Learn In This Chapter:

- ✓ What are social stories
- ✓ How to create the most effective social stories
- ✓ How to teach new behaviors with amazing results using social stories - simple 4 step system
- ✓ Social Stories Do's and Don'ts

◆ ◆ ◆ ◆ ◆ ◆ ◆ ◆ ◆ ◆ ◆ ◆ ◆ ◆ ◆ ◆ ◆

Social stories can actually be quite common. Sometimes you even see them in libraries and bookstores. But what I'm walking you through here is beyond "get a social story". I will explain to you the elements that make a good social story, and most importantly, I'll show you my simple *four-step system for social stories* so you know how to get amazing results from social stories.

What are Social Stories?
How do we teach a desired Behavior? We use social stories. Social stories are visual stories developed to teach special needs children (and all children) behaviors, skills, interactions, situations, and concepts. They are stories with a specific skill, concept or behavior that is put into a book format for a child to read and learn about. They can be very effective in new behavior teaching when the child reads it several times a day. Individualizing it for your child would ensure the closest match to your child's needs.

How to Create the Most Effective Social Stories
There are many ways to create social stories. What I'm teaching you here is not the only way to create it, but it is, from my experience, the way to make the most effective social stories for the best behavior learning results.

I will give you an example so you can understand how to make the most impactful social stories for your child. The steps to creating a social story are:

    A. planning and creating the plot and the visuals,
    B. putting the physical book together

A. Planning and Creating the Plot and the Visuals:

As an example, my child always tends to shut down or have a tantrum when he's faced with a very difficult task. So I wanted to make a social story that talked about what to do when things get difficult. I broke the story plot into three parts, which are usually the three pages of the story (it could also be four pages sometimes). The three parts are:

Part one (page 1): the situation about which you are trying to teach --
Here I'm trying to teach about what happens when things get hard. So, on page one I say "sometimes things are difficult". And my visual aid for this page includes pictures of things that my child does in his life that are difficult for him or pictures of things that represent difficult tasks. For example, I will have a picture of a man looking up the mountain that is very high and hard to climb. And I will have a picture of my child trying to ride on the bike for the first time. At the time my child was going through this lesson he was in karate which was extremely difficult for him, so I had a picture of a person or it could be himself in karate and I also had a picture of a student trying to do homework with a puzzled face. The intent of this page is show that sometimes things get hard and you have quite a few visual aids to represent and to convey the idea of a hard and difficult task. You have to be very visual about your book because children on the Spectrum work very well with visual representations and that is the only way they can get a real picture of what is going on.

Part two (page 2): the behavior expected in that situation --
Part two/page two would state the behavior expected of your child in that situation. For example, when things get difficult, I would like for him to ask for help. So what I say in this page is "when things get hard I ask for help". My visual aid in this page includes a picture of my child happily asking for help.

Do I have to or need to use my child's actual picture? The answer depends on the child because some children prefer seeing pictures of themselves while others prefer seeing General pictures of stick figures, or characters. The other consideration is that pictures of your own child may sometimes take longer to collect if you have to take a picture get a good shot printed and then include into your book. Sometimes it's better to have the book and start reading it and learning from it than to not have the book because you're waiting for the perfect picture.

Remember that you have to keep it very simple. The only thing here that you are trying to convey in this page is the behavior of asking for help. Therefore your one-liner includes only something about asking for help and your picture includes only a child asking for help.

Part 3 page 3: the conclusion - a positive note.
In my social stories, I like to end the stories with a positive note. In the last part of the plot it is usually

something positive that happens when a child does the behavior you want. For example, continuing with my social story book "when something gets hard", the conclusion of my book will say something like "Mama and papa are proud of me when I ask for help", or I could also say "I am proud of myself when I ask for help". Another idea is to say "I can get help when I ask for help". Whatever you say, leave on a positive note, stating the positive feeling your child would experience should he/she choose the desired behavior.

Sometimes you can break out the results of the behavior into two portions. For example, page 3 may say "I can get help when I ask for help" and page 4 may say "mama and papa are proud of me when I ask for help."

B. Putting the Physical Book Together

One way to put the physical book together is to make it electronically, using programs such as PowerPoint or whatever graphing programs you are comfortable using. Then print the pages out and laminate the pages, and bind it together with a ring, or whichever way you choose to bind it.

Another choice is to hand draw and handwrite all the pages, laminate the pages, and bind them. You could also staple the pages together as a simple way of binding them.

You may have noticed that social stories are actually everywhere. There are social stories even in children's libraries, for instance, a book about manners. Some of them are marvelous and are great reads to increase a child's awareness. Typically, the books you find in libraries or bookstores are far more complex than what I'm teaching you to create here, which is the reason I'm teaching you to make your own. While those library or bookstore social story books are wonderful, what I'm teaching you to target here is a new behavior/skill acquisition in its simplest form, fostered through the simplest and extremely targeted form of social story book. For this purpose, we want to keep it simple, so the child can get the point easily, especially since we are targeting a new skill/behavior acquisition here.

Surely it doesn't stop at creating the social story. The most important part of social story is how you use it and how you make social stories work effectively. This is where you are going to see amazing results.

How to Teach New Behaviors with Amazing Results Using Social Stories – a Simple 4 Step System

As stated above, the key is what you do with the social story that determines the results you get from it. Here I'm teaching you, step by step, the specific ways to use them so you can flourish with amazing results. Once you have the social stories made, follow my simple *four-step system for social stories* below:

1. **Step 1: Read it a many times.**
   You want to read it with your child several times a day in the beginning of teaching a new behavior, concept, skill, or situation. Your goal is to read it so many times that it starts becoming a second nature reaction for

your child to behave that way in those situations. They first have to read it over and over again until they start forming new neural pathways in their brain about, for example, what to do when things get hard – "ask for help". First, set a goal to read it together at least three times a day.

2. **Step 2: Frequent deliberate practice.**
   In addition to repeatedly reading the story several times a day, you also need to deliberately create frequent opportunities to practice that skill. Set a goal to practice the skill at least once a day. This is when you deliberately create a situation that matches the situation in your social story, and teach/practice with your child to use the skill he or she learned in the social story. Again, using the example of my "what to do when things get hard" story, at least one time a day, I purposely present my child with a difficult task to practice the skill of asking for help in that situation.

   How do you practice? Initially, prior to presenting him with a difficult task, I would read the social story with him once. Immediately after the reading, I would give him a heads up "I'm going to ask you to do something very hard next. And what do you do when things get hard?" Child should respond "ask for help". Say "Great, let's practice that now". Present him with a difficult task and if your child doesn't yet ask for help by himself, you prompt him to say "help please". As soon as he says it, and especially the first time he says it, bring on your full-blown cheerleader team, which consists of yourself plus a firework-like energy of excitement – go all out, cheer for him! Now he got the reinforcement that "help please" is what he is supposed to say when things get hard. Immediately, present him with another difficult task and work towards him initiating the desired/taught behavior on his own.

If possible, repeat this process a few times during the same sitting. Remember, practice makes perfect. It is true for riding a bike, swimming, for a baby learning how to walk for the first time, and it is also true for learning a new behavior. If you are unable to reproduce the same practice round several times during that one sitting, it is perfectly fine – it is NOT an all-or-nothing deal. Instead, your results build on an accumulation of your successful practices. The higher amount and the more frequent the practice the faster the skill acquisition.

Continue to read your social story book several times a day throughout step 2 phase (and through all steps of this system). You are continuing to build a second nature element in your child's brain for this new behavior/skill by reading it over and over again.

3. **Step 3: Spontaneous Practice.**
Your child is ready for this third step after he or she has had a series of successes in Step 2: *frequent deliberate practice*. You want to make sure he or she can successfully perform the new behavior/skill without any prompting before proceeding to step three.

What is the difference between a *deliberate* practice and a *spontaneous* practice?

In step 2: Frequent deliberate practice, we tell the child that we are about to practice "what to do when things get hard", and we do this immediately after we read the social story. We deliberately create the situations to give practices, and we practice it several times in a row (in one sitting).

In Step 3: Spontaneous Practice, we do not tell the child that we are about to practice "what to do when things get hard", we practice spontaneously. After your child has had repeated success with step 2, you tell him/her "a few times today, I'm going to ask you to do something hard. And whenever I ask you to do something hard, what do you do?" Your child should respond "Ask for help!" By now your child should know this answer very well, but the challenge now is doing so without the advance warning we gave in step 2. Offer a reward for your child, "If you can ask for help every time I ask you to do something hard, you will get to ___" (something rewarding for your child).

Next, sometime during the day, go to your child and say "remember I said I was going to ask you to do something hard a few times today? Well, now is the time!" Present your child with a difficult task and once again celebrate his/her success in performing the desired behavior.

Your celebration of success and your burst of energy feeding into his or her success is what is going to maintain, or even increase, this desired behavior from your child. Therefore, under no circumstance should you back down by even a small notch in your cheerleading effort – your positive and dramatic reaction here is far too critical to your child's success. Even if you are tired and just don't have the energy to be head-to-toe excited over his or her new behavior here, FAKE IT! You can't afford not to! Repeat this procedure as many times a day as you can.

After a while, you can stop reminding him/her with "remember I said I was going to ask you to do something hard?" Start phasing the reminders out and making it increasingly more spontaneous. Again, keep your cheerleading squad EVERY TIME he/she has a success.

Still, continue to read your social story book several times a day throughout the step 3 period.

4. **Step 4: Cheer a lot and never stop cheering.**
   This is when you go live with your child's new skill. After your child can have predictable success in step 3, you are in step 4 where the goal is for your child to be able to perform the behavior any time the situation occurs, especially outside of home or outside of your step 2 and step 3 practice environments. Use of that new skill in life is the goal here. This is when your child is working towards mastery, or second nature behavior. In this step you want to seek out opportunities to help your

child be successful at using his or her new skill in those random situations that come up in his everyday life.

At every success, cheer like there is no tomorrow! When can we be done cheering? Let's think for a minute. Your every effort through every step in this chapter helped your child form a desirable new skill/behavior, and your excitement in his/her success is what is maintaining his successes. If you don't want his success in this new behavior/skill to stop, then you don't want to stop what's maintaining that success – your energy and emotion in his successes. You never want to be done cheering for your child's success. You want your child to know that you are always excited about his victories.

You can start decreasing the number of times per day that you read the social story as you see some skill acquisition through the process of step 3. But you never want to completely stop reading the social story until your child has completely mastered the new skills to the point of it being second nature. This will take a while to accomplish as behavior change is a process. Any time after the true mastery of a skill, if you ever start seeing a regression (could be due to various reasons), you want to bring your social story book back out for review, and even do some practices for review. However, with step 4 – cheer a lot and never stop cheering, you should have little reason to experience regression. Your cheering will be maintaining this new desirable behavior the same way your negative emotions can maintain an undesirable behavior to the point of it being a real challenge.

Dos and Don't with Social Story

- Do Be simple and precise in your story.
- Do Be visual (use simple illustrations or pictures to convey ideas)
- Do Be positive in your conclusion.
- Do Make your reading a pleasant event – associate this new skill with a pleasant feeling
- Do have discussions about your book reading – expand the context of their understanding
- Do practice a lot, and then even more
- Don't make reading a punishment or a chore
- Don't ever stop cheering

Your Take-Away From This Chapter:

✓ Teach new behaviors using this simple four-step social story system
✓ Deliberately create opportunities to practice the new behavior
✓ Use success strategies and the power of your words to reinforce new behaviors until it becomes second nature

Section IV - Transforming External Behaviors: Reaping the Fruit

CHAPTER 12
The 3 Letters that Demystify Behaviors

♦ ♦ ♦ ♦ ♦ ♦ ♦ ♦ ♦ ♦ ♦ ♦ ♦ ♦ ♦

What You Will Learn In This Chapter:

- ✓ Behavioral language - what is behavior ABC
- ✓ The 4 primary functions of behavior
- ✓ How to gain important information you can use to modify a behavior by analyzing functions and the ABCs of a behavior
- ✓ Making a behavioral plan

♦ ♦ ♦ ♦ ♦ ♦ ♦ ♦ ♦ ♦ ♦ ♦ ♦ ♦ ♦

What is the behavior ABC?

In the Applied Behavior Analysis field, ABC are the three fundamental elements used to analyze and change difficult behaviors. ABC refers to Antecedent, Behavior, and Consequence.

A: Antecedent -- The antecedent is the setting prior to the behavior ("target behavior"); it's something that may contribute to the target behavior. Examples of antecedent: a change in environment, a request to the child to do something, the presence or action of another person around the child. To find the A for a target behavior, simply ask "What was happening just before the target behavior? Is there something that might have triggered the behavior?"

B: Behavior -- The problem behavior, which we also call the "target behavior".

C: Consequence -- What happens immediately after the target behavior - the outcome of the target behavior? The Consequence is what reinforces the behavior. For every behavior there is something that is maintaining that behavior (keeping the behavior happening); we call the element that maintains the behavior the reinforcer, or the consequence.

There are two types of reinforcers, positive and negative. Positive reinforcers are things you add to the environment to increase the desired behavior. After you consistently and repeatedly apply the positive reinforcers, an increase in the behavior follows. Examples of positive reinforcers are tokens, games food items, stickers. Negative reinforcers are aversive things you remove from the environment to increase the desired behavior. For example, if you tell your child 'If you finish your work by 2 pm today, you won't have to take out the trash, you have removed the aversive chore (taking out the trash) to reinforce the desired behavior of finishing his work on time.

An example of the ABC (Figure 12-1):

Every time the child is asked to clean up, he hits someone. He then gets put into time-out. The A (Antecedent) is the request to clean, because the hitting behavior always happens right after he is asked to clean, and it is triggered by the request to clean. The B (Behavior) is the target behavior of hitting. The C (Consequence) is time-out, in which case the child doesn't have to clean anymore because he is in time-out. So if the child is asked to clean up, if the child hits, he no longer has to clean up. Do you see why every time the child is asked to clean he hits someone? Because he has very successfully gotten out of the chore of cleaning by hitting someone - he has successfully *escaped* the task of cleaning. Do you see how the C (Consequence) of time-out in this scenario is exactly what is maintaining ("reinforcing") the target behavior of hitting? For as long as he hits someone, he will get out of having to clean - surely he will hit every time he is asked to clean. Pretty simple from the child's perspective.

ABC's of Behavior Chart

A Antecedent	B Behavior	C Consequence	Function
What Happened Before the Behavior	What the Child Did	What Happened After the Behavior	What Function Does this Behavior Serve?
Request to Clean	Hitting	Time out (doesn't need to clean)	Escape (from cleaning)

© 2017 Harmonious Clan

Figure 12-1 Example ABC's of Behavior Chart

Functions of Behavior

Speaking of this child avoiding the task of cleaning, there is a purpose behind every behavior. The purpose of the hitting behavior in this scenario is to avoid something (to escape from having to clean up). When you analyze a behavior, you want to find out the purpose of a behavior, which we call the "function" of a behavior.

There are **4 primary functions of a behavior** that maintain the behavior:

1) **Attention** - get attention from someone
2) **Access** - get access to something the child desires
3) **Escape** - avoid something; avoid a situation or avoid having to do something
4) **Sensory stimulation** - it satisfies their sensory needs and feels good to them. (This is why in this book we

have dealt with meeting the sensory needs far before we address the behavior).

You need to analyze the situation with your ABC chart (as shown in **Figure 12- 1** above) to figure out if the child's behavior has served the function. Compare your A (Antecedent) against your C (Consequence) to see if the behavior has served a purpose. In this example, the A is request to clean and the C is don't need to clean - the child went from request-to-clean (A) to don't-need-to-clean (C) by exhibiting the behavior of hitting (B). In other words, if your child gets from A to C by exhibiting his B, then **his B is serving _the function_ of his behavior**; _he is very successful at getting from A to his desired C using this B, and he will absolutely continue to utilize this B to get him from A to C!_ Wouldn't you keep doing what works, too? This particular behavior is being "reinforced".

How do I figure out the function of a behavior?
Formulate the hypothesis:

1. Observe the behavior and write down what happens before and immediately after the behavior.
2. Look for patterns that help identify the function of the behavior; the functions of behavior are listed below (Attention, Access, Escape, Sensory Stimulation)
    a. What happens before the behavior will indicate driving functions
    b. What happens after the behavior clues us in to the maintaining variables (reinforcers)

Test out the hypothesis:

1) <u>Attention</u> - what happens to the behavior if you give your child your undivided attention? If the behavior disappears then the function of the behavior is to get attention.
2) <u>Access</u> - what happens to the behavior if you give your child his preferred object? If the behavior disappears then the function of the behavior is to gain access.
3) <u>Escape</u> - what happens to the behavior if you remove the demand that you placed onto the child? If the behavior disappears then the function of the behavior is to escape.
4) <u>Sensory Stimulation</u> - what happens to the behavior if you provide that sensory stimulation for the child? If the behavior disappears then the function of the behavior is to gain sensory stimulation.

Replacement Behaviors

Replacement behavior is the desired behavior you would like your child to exhibit instead of the original target behavior (the problematic behavior). When you figure out the ABC and the function of the behavior, you want to define and work towards a replacement behavior.

For example, If your child is yelling to get your attention every time you get on the phone with someone, your A is absence of attention (you getting on the phone), your B is yelling, your C is getting attention, and the function of this behavior is attention. In this case, your replacement behavior might be something like, tap on my shoulder and calmly say "excuse me".

You want to teach this replacement behavior and reinforce this replacement behavior.

How do you find a replacement behavior? A good replacement behavior will successfully serve the same function as the original target behavior. In this example, the replacement behavior of tapping on my shoulder and calmly saying "excuse me" will serve the same function of getting my attention. A good replacement behavior should also be orthogonal to the target behavior, meaning while your child is exhibiting the replacement behavior, he will not be able to exhibit the target behavior simultaneously. In this example, your child can't possibly be tapping on your shoulder calmly saying "excuse me" while yelling at the same time.

Define a replacement behavior, teach it, and reinforce it, so you will get more of it.

Make a Behavior Plan

Once you figure out the function of the behavior and have successfully analyzed a specific behavior's ABC, then you can make a plan to modify the behavior. You can change or eliminate the A (Antecedent). By modifying the antecedents and the environment, you are changing or eliminating the A, such that you can have the opportunity to reinforce the desirable (replacement behavior).

As a parent, you need to have a plan like this in place so that any minute when the difficult behavior comes up, you already know ahead of time just what you would do and that you are not going to resort to screaming, yelling, or punishing the child out of irrational anger. You need this plan to keep you sane and to be effective in handling your child's behavior, because as you already know, difficult behaviors can be very difficult sometimes, especially when your child has a tested and proven-to-work B in mind.

To summarize this chapter, analyze the ABC and the function of a problem behavior. After your analysis, find a replacement behavior to teach and reinforce. Lastly create a behavior plan for yourself so you can remain calm, in control, and highly effective at diminishing your child's problem behaviors.

Food for thought on various methods of dealing with behaviors - so what's your take?

Some extra thoughts to ponder about the paths someone might choose to take upon the engagement of a child's problem behavior - you can:

1) Ignore it
   "Extinction" in behavior science is used to describe situations when you no longer provide a reinforcer for a previously reinforced behavior. In plain English, you are essentially ignoring the behavior. For a behavior maintained by <u>attention</u>, ignoring the behavior is "extinction". Here is a significant caveat for implementing a planned ignoring technique – the behavior *WILL increase* before it decreases. The behavior can increase at double the rate and intensity before it decreases. This is just the natural curve for "extinction" (ignoring).

That said, the important thing is that you stick to the ignoring and block anything that can be harmful.

While ignoring may sometimes be truly the most effective way to diminish a problem behavior, since you are essentially disallowing the behavior to serve its function, ignoring sometimes may not be feasible due to safety and other concerns.

In situations where you can ignore the behavior, ignore it, but, as I stated before, be careful not to ignore it for a while and then give in at the last minute. A simple example is when a parent ignores a child's whine or tantrum at the store to get the toy they want, and the parent ignores the tantrum for a good 25 minutes until he or she finally can't put up with it and decides to buy it for the child. Who wins? The child! And what are you teaching the child to do? To tantrum for NO LESS THAN 25 minutes because 25 minutes is your break-down point! I'm sure out-lasting you in this fashion is not what you want to teach your child, so if you choose to ignore, make sure you know what you are signing up for and be absolutely certain that YOU will be the one to out-last your child.

2) Punishment
Punishment can increase the undesirable behavior by drawing attention (wanted or unwanted attention) to the problem behavior. In my opinion and my experience, ideas in my "success paradigm" chapters are far more effective, long-lasting, and empowering to the child than punishment.

3) Find a replacement behavior
You draw attention to the desired behavior and you get to reinforce the desired behavior. It is many times the best choice as a hands-on, in the moment, dealing of problem behaviors.

Want a booster shot on replacement behavior? From my experience, using replacement behaviors as an in-the-moment implementation in combination with the powerful strategies from the "success paradigm" as a philosophy and day-to-day way of seeing and treating your child, is most effective, most empowering, and most innate to the child.

◆ ◆ ◆ ◆ ◆ ◆ ◆ ◆ ◆ ◆ ◆ ◆ ◆ ◆ ◆ ◆ ◆

Your Take-Away From This Chapter:

✓ Use what you learned from this chapter (the behavior ABC, functions of behaviors, etc.) to treat the specific behavior, and use the "paradigm shift" to treat your child.

✓ Treat your child like he is a success!

◆ ◆ ◆ ◆ ◆ ◆ ◆ ◆ ◆ ◆ ◆ ◆ ◆ ◆ ◆ ◆ ◆

CHAPTER 13
The Remedy for Unplugging Power Struggles

♦ ♦ ♦ ♦ ♦ ♦ ♦ ♦ ♦ ♦ ♦ ♦ ♦ ♦ ♦

What You Will Learn In This Chapter:

- ✓ What's behind control issues and power struggles?
- ✓ How to minimize power struggles and maximize compliance when your child is trying to take control of the situation

♦ ♦ ♦ ♦ ♦ ♦ ♦ ♦ ♦ ♦ ♦ ♦ ♦ ♦ ♦

My two boys are running through the living room and jumping through the roof turning the house upside down. If you ever had an athletic dog that you trapped in the house the whole day, you will know what I mean - time to let the dogs out and get some energy out before your dog chews up everything in your house. This is where I was with my two oldest boys just a minute ago. I also know that if I tell them to go exercise or run off some energy outside they would flat out deny the need to and we'd have a power struggle over whether or not they should be exercising outside or playing inside at this time. So I never even mentioned it. I secretly called the two of them to me (secret from all the rest of the clan) and whispered, "We're all going to get some exercise next. But I wonder what your two preferences are - would you like to go together just the two of you or one at a time taking turns?" They immediately responded "we want to go together!" "Great! You'll have fun with just the two of you and no younger siblings". The next question of preference is, "would you like to run together or jump on the trampoline together or do both?" After a 20 second discussion amongst themselves they replied "We want to run 5 laps and then do trampoline together". I said "awesome, off you go!" My wild dog problem of having to drop what they are doing and get some exercise is now solved with much success and cheerful "compliance". Had I told them to go exercise I would have placed myself right in the middle of a control issue, which some parents call a "power struggle".

It's an art to get your child to do "as you say". Sometimes you get a feeling that a child or a certain stage of a child is just so difficult and stubborn that it almost seems like his sole purpose of existence is to make your life difficult. This can happen if your child is having some control issues.

Control Issues and Power Struggles

Control issues can be very common in children, especially Children with SDN. Due to their sensory processing integration issues and various sensitivities, their internal systems feel very much out of control because their internal state is absolutely chaotic and unmanageable. When they feel out of control internally they feel and act out of control externally as well. This is how they feel: all kinds of things are just "happening to me" and I don't have any control or say over anything that "happens to me" and my life. In attempt to regain control (which is much needed for the child) and put every piece of the chaos back in order, the child tends to exhibit behaviors to take control over the situation. This can very much feel like and look like Oppositional Defiance, basically, being oppositional and defiant with everything you say just to gain control over the situation.

A recent example of this is when we had to switch therapist and bring in a new therapist. Our son started acting with much defiance in every area of his life, basically making the statement that "I did not ask this person to come here and tell me what to do. I don't want her here, but I have no control over it. I need some control in my life. I need a say in my own life and I'm going to have it!" That message is so clear to me based on his behaviors. He proceeded to insist a say in every part of his life and that means he was oppositional with me in every corner. What was my fix?

Put the focus on what your child has control over

Of course there is adjustment and transition to a new person to take into consideration, but on the control issue, I "showed" my son how there are things that we cannot control and there are things that we can control. I say I "showed" because I showed him all the times when he has control and has choices. I "put the control back into his hands" so he didn't feel such a desperate need to control things when he needed to comply. I did so by giving him plenty of choices and options over just about everything I could allow. She (the new therapist) is going to be here, which we cannot control, but you get to choose what you would like to do BEFORE you see her, you get to choose what you would like to do AFTER you are done with her, and you even get the pick your choice of snack to have WHILE you work with her because it's ok to eat then. It's all your choice. I'm putting the focus and attention on what the child does have control over.

On a regular basis, offer as many choices and options as you can. You do this to:

1) Train your child how to make choices when faced with decisions and options
2) Give your child the control he needs in his life

The two types of areas where you can give choices and options are:

a) <u>Things that the child CAN control (as opposed to things that he/she CANNOT control).</u>

For example, "We are going to do this homework assignment, and you get to choose if you'd like to do it on the paper or the computer." So you put no attention on the what the child CANNOT control - the child has no control over having to do this assignment. Instead, you place the focus on the items that he/she CAN control - do I want to do it on paper or the computer?

This also teaches a child a very valuable lesson in life - "Be flexible over what I cannot control; take charge over things I can control."

b) All the things that don't matter.

Would you like the pink sweater or the white seater? What flavor would you like? What would you like to use? Would you like a tiger toothbrush or a frog toothbrush? There are all kinds of things that really don't matter where you are probably already giving your child the say. What I'm suggesting is that you see if there is anywhere else where you can offer an option and offer it, and make sure you present it to the child in a fashion which leaves them with the feeling that they have an abundance of options, choices, and control in their own lives.

On matters where your child with SDN struggles to comply, but must meet the requirement, you want to make an extra effort to identify elements around that big requirement that your child can have control over.

For example, if your child fights over having to clean his room, he can't get out of having to clean his room but give him as much control over elements within the requirement to clean the room - "Would you like to do it before or after lunch?" "Would you like to straighten up the desk first or the closet first?" "Would you like to clean with music on or without music on?" "Would you like to be by yourself while you clean or would you like me to keep you company?"..... the options goes on if you think about it. Present to your child a couple or a few (if not overwhelming) areas where he can control and invite him to be in the driver's seat for his preferences.

When my little girl insists on wearing a single layered cute top when it's 10 degrees outside, I lay out 2-3 cute sweaters and ask "Would you like the polka dot sweater or the pink-and-white sweater over your top?

Start with no more than 2 options for every decision you present to a child under the age of 6. As your child matures and is capable of handling more options without delaying the decision and delaying the execution on the request, it's ok to give more than 2 options, but you may find it easier to keep things simple.

Having options and the ability to make choices is so liberating to a child with SDN. It helps them feel in control and confident. And what's in it for you is the diminishing power struggle you have to deal with, and a far more cooperative child.

Your Take-Away From This Chapter:

- ✓ Give your child the power and control on the insignificant things whenever possible (0% of the time)
- ✓ Create an environment where the child feels reasonably in control rather than "not in control" or like he "never has a say"
- ✓ During the 20% of the time your child MUST do things your way, your child isn't so desperate to defy you because he has a say most other times

CHAPTER 14

The Ultimate System to Ignite a Child's Self-Motivation

◆ ◆ ◆ ◆ ◆ ◆ ◆ ◆ ◆ ◆ ◆ ◆ ◆ ◆ ◆ ◆

What You Will Learn In This Chapter:

- ✓ What is Token system and why does it matter
- ✓ Misconceptions about token systems
- ✓ How to implement an effective token system

◆ ◆ ◆ ◆ ◆ ◆ ◆ ◆ ◆ ◆ ◆ ◆ ◆ ◆ ◆ ◆

What is a Token System and Why Does It Matter

A token system is a system that allows a child to enjoy the fruit of his/her hard work. It is a system that credits the child for every good deed he does and allows the child to exchange the credit he earns for appropriate objects and privileges that he desires.

A token system serves the child in several ways:

1) **Demonstrates your appreciation for your child's successes or good efforts in practical actions and tangible ways**
   I have discussed with you a great deal about the importance of your acknowledgement to your child's every little success and effort. You as the parent, teacher, or caregiver are a crucial figure in your child's life. It is not only important that your child knows that you notice his efforts and good actions, but that you verbally acknowledge him, pour out your emotional energy to him, AND at the end of the day, you show your appreciation to him in a practical, tangible way.

   Have you ever done an outstanding job at work and had a boss who gave you a lot of verbal acknowledgement, praises, or even a nice plaque with your name and your accomplishments on it, made you the "employee of the month", but just didn't actually give you a raise in your salary or a one-time bonus? At the end of the day, what is all that worth to you when you can't see it reflect in your bottom line – a bigger paycheck, ability to afford a better lifestyle, a bonus, or a simple gift card? To say all the nice things to your child about his great work or great effort and not give him something tangible feels a little bit like this job situation. You start wondering if your employer actually appreciates you or if he/she is just saying it because "words are cheap". It is great that you have given plenty of verbal acknowledgements and positive emotional energy to your child for his good deeds, and now it's time to top it off with something tangible – a tangible object or privilege that your child can enjoy.

2) **Gives the child the experience of a societal economy**
Isn't this how it works in the real society? You work hard or you add value, you earn money, you buy things you need and want with your hard earned money. This system has existed since history – you hunt, you farm, you get food; you don't hunt, don't farm, you don't get food. A token system is a very realistic model of how the society works and how the economy system works. It gives your child a taste of reality in life. By working hard your child earns something to enjoy. The amount of things/privileges you earn is proportion to the effort you put in. In the same way at home, the more effort your child puts into desirable behaviors the more credits he earns and the more goodies he gets – it's simple. Eventually your child can even learn the concept of choice between saving my credits (money) for the bigger things later, or spending my credits (money) for the small thing I want right now.

3) **Gives the child a personal reason to work hard**
One of the toughest things for many Children with SDN is motivation. There is so much going on inside of them that most things are much harder than they are to children without the sensitivity and divergent needs. In many situations, they really need a personal reason

to push through it and give it their effort. If they know what they are working towards (a tangible item), it can help overcome the resistance to do what's difficult.

Token System Misconceptions

1) **"You are bribing the child, and that's wrong"**
The dictionary definition of "bribe" is to "persuade someone to act in one's favor, typically illegally or dishonestly, by a gift of money or other inducement", and we are not talking about that here. What I'm suggesting here is not illegal, dishonest, or with an ill agenda. What I'm suggesting here is to show your appreciation for your child's good work in practical terms in addition to verbal acknowledgement.

A second fact is – no one works for free. As an adult, you don't work for free, even when you volunteer and don't get paid money, for example, you get something in return – a satisfaction that you have helped someone, a satisfaction that somebody's life is better because of what you did. Anytime you put in your effort, you expect something in return, even if it's just plain joy, then you expect joy. Rarely do people do things when they don't get anything out of it. In that case, why would anyone expect a child to do something (especially things that are difficult for them – e.g. behave in a way you want them to behave) and receive nothing in return? Even in relationships, things are often reciprocal – without reciprocation where both parties put in something and both parties get something out of it, one party may drop out of the relationship due to lack of satisfaction and lack of engagement from the other party.

A token system is not only a practical show of your appreciation of your child's success, it is also an encouragement to do more of the good behavior. This form of encouragement (to ask people to get out of their way and do something) is used widely in our society. For example, most businesses have some sort of customer reward program to encourage your continuous and frequent purchase of their products or acquisition of their services (buy 3, get the 4th free). Most libraries have a summer reading program that gives you rewards and incentives to read more. Many modern pediatric dentistry practices give a child a small prize for their cooperation and their visit, as they realize that dentist visits can be difficult for some children. It's a pretty standard practice that pediatricians give young children stickers after they get vaccinated. One of my favorite eateries recently started a customer reward program, and suddenly I'm there that many more times a month. You are using the same method to encourage your child to do more of the good behavior. And who doesn't love rewards? There is nothing wrong with that; in fact you are teaching children the concept of earning what they want, which they are going to have to understand one day when they want that eighty-thousand dollar car.

2) **"The child won't work or do anything if there is no reward"**
It is absolutely true that you don't want your child to become accustomed to the idea of "what's in it for

me?" and not do anything if they don't get anything out of it. Your possible fear is that having a token system that rewards your child for good deeds will prevent your child from doing the right things when the visible reward is not present. However, that won't likely happen if you do it right.

The child may need a kick-start (the reward in the token system) as a reason to do it when you are asking them to do something new and difficult. After steady achievement of the desired behavior over a certain amount of time, you want to phase out the reward and maintain the desired behavior and you are certainly able to. Put it this way, many parents give young children a treat every time they have successfully used the toilet when they are first being toilet trained. And how many adults do you know that won't use the toilet properly when not offered a treat? Probably none. That goes to tell you how an incentive is helpful (at times possibly needed) to learn a new behavior, but once the behavior is learned and mastered, it is possible for the learned behavior to maintain when naturally occurring reinforcers in the natural environment take over and the programmed consequence is no longer needed. It becomes a second nature.

So no worries about this, but yes, just from an attitude perspective you do want to teach your child not to get into the mentality of "what do I get" for everything he is asked to do - some things are just the right thing to do and that's why we do them. However, it takes time and maturity to get to that point. In the very beginning of a brand new behavioral demand that is a challenge to a child, incentives are helpful and in some cases needed. And don't forget, the other side of the story is that you really want to show your child your appreciation for his smallest effort, because he needs to know that what he does matters to you.

How to Implement an Effective Token System

1) **Create the platform to track the earned credits**
   Start off by creating a platform for which to track your child's earned credits. It can be a sheet, a piece of paper, whiteboard, or a chart. It just needs to be a place where you track how much credit your child has earned. If you choose not to track it that way, you can even give your child an actual physical token (like physical money) every time he exhibits the desired behavior, and have your child collect the tokens to exchange for a reward after a defined amount of token credit or time.

2) **Define behaviors that can earn tokens**
   Decide the desirable behaviors that you want to work on and acknowledge. Discuss what those behaviors are with your child. Write and/or illustrate them visually for your child so he always knows how he can earn his tokens.

3) **Create a menu of rewards**
   Find out what objects and privileges your child finds desirable; if appropriate, provide those objects and privileges as rewards for earning a certain amount of tokens.

Examples of rewards could be objects, such as small toys, interesting novelty items, a food or drink that is out of their ordinary daily consumption and therefore is considered "special" to them, stickers if they like them, fun items or supplies for arts and crafts, an item they really wanted, basically, anything they find interesting. A reward could also be in the form of a privilege, such as extra screen time for movies, video games, shopping trips, any special trips or out-of-ordinary activities.

The reward needs to be something beyond the ordinary "basics" that you provide to them as caregivers. For example, in the case of objects, as the caregiver you already provide them with basic school supplies such as pencils (which is considered a "basic"), but if they want that shimmery bendable pencil with a race car model on the top they saw at the store, that "upgrade" can be earned as a reward. As caregivers you provide them with all their meals, but if they want, say, ice cream or dessert, which is not a nutritional requirement for a fundamental meal, they can earn that "upgrade" to their "basic" meal as their reward (provided you allow that special food they want, of course). They may have free time or playtime every day, but to go go-carting or to go to the movies for their free/play time can be an "upgrade" to their playtime that they can "earn". In other words, with their earned tokens, they get to "enhance" their life.

In your menu, you also need to set your "price" — decide how much credit (how many tokens) will buy you what kind of reward. For children who are too young to truly comprehend the concept of "value", you may want to make all the choices equal price and keep it simple – anytime you get x tokens, you can pick anything from the menu.

4) **Give your child tokens/credits**
Now that everything about the token system is in place, you just need to start giving out the tokens. Be very diligent about giving your child credit for any good deeds, for any little successes or things that you define as ways to earn tokens, that is, catch your child being good, give your verbal acknowledgement, give your enthusiasm in your emotional energy, and lastly, give your appreciation in "real pay" – tokens! Don't slack off on your verbal and emotional energy just because you have tokens to give now – You've got to keep up with your verbal acknowledgement and enthusiasm for your child, you are just adding to their "bottom line", their "paycheck" now on top of all the rest.

◆ ◆ ◆ ◆ ◆ ◆ ◆ ◆ ◆ ◆ ◆ ◆ ◆ ◆ ◆ ◆

Your Take-Away From This Chapter:

- ✓ It is especially difficult for a child with Sensitive Divergent Needs to get out of their comfort zone and perform a new task
- ✓ Teach new behaviors by using the token system strategies learned here

◆ ◆ ◆ ◆ ◆ ◆ ◆ ◆ ◆ ◆ ◆ ◆ ◆ ◆ ◆ ◆

CHAPTER 15
The Single Action That Stops Behaviors in Their Tracks

♦ ♦ ♦ ♦ ♦ ♦ ♦ ♦ ♦ ♦ ♦ ♦ ♦ ♦ ♦ ♦

What You Will Learn In This Chapter:

- ✓ The two sides to work in to eliminate difficult behaviors
- ✓ The price for good behaviors
- ✓ Fueling your child's success to eliminate difficult behaviors

♦ ♦ ♦ ♦ ♦ ♦ ♦ ♦ ♦ ♦ ♦ ♦ ♦ ♦ ♦ ♦

One of the most important pieces of advice I can give you when it comes to difficult undesirable behaviors is: don't even let it happen! And you're wondering – "what do you mean don't even let it happen? Of course, I would never let that behavior happen if I could help it." What I mean is that you need to do everything in your power to avoid it or prevent it, AND work it from the other side at the same time. What other side?

Work the Two Sides
What are the two sides that you need to work simultaneously?

1) Slam on the gas pedal to fuel the desire to do right,
2) Avoid or prevent the undesirable behaviors
   a. **support**
   b. **don't even let it happen!**

Some of the more difficult behaviors are much harder to deal with once the child gets into the pattern of such undesirable behaviors. Therefore, you want to do everything you can to avoid the undesirable behavior. But just that alone will not work. The other side of it is that you have to slam on your gas pedal and **fuel** the desirable behaviors like there is no tomorrow. In doing so, you can diminish the undesirable behaviors and more, replace them with desirable behaviors.

1) How do you fuel the desire to do right?
You do so by using my previously suggested strategies including creating little successes, having verbal acknowledgement, paradigm shift for the child, etc. All of those chapters prior to this one do need to come first. Then when you get to the actual difficult behaviors you have to just avoid it/prevent it until that behavior dissipates. Meanwhile, you are building up on the positives. You are building up the child's level of confidence. You are building up the child's self-perception,

so that he or she will be striving to be on fire to do the right things.

2) How do you avoid or prevent the undesirable behaviors?
My first example for you comes from a dog trainer. Caveat: I do NOT suggest that you treat your child like a dog. I have the absolute most respect for your child as a human being and for any children with or without special needs. Therefore, the idea isn't to treat your child like a dog in a negative sense, but rather to make a point about behavior science to help illustrate my "Don't even let it happen" strategy.

The very first time I had a puppy years ago, one of the biggest problems was the puppy urinating in the house. I did not know enough to understand how to fix that behavior. The dog trainer said that you just have to not let it happen and I thought, "What do you mean not let it happen? He lifts up his leg and starts urinating. How can I not let it happen?" The answer is twofold:

A. Support - For example, for a brand new puppy who does not have enough bladder control and does not know that he's not supposed to go to the restroom in the house, you need to take the dog out every 15 minutes or 30 minutes to empty the bladder. What you are doing here is providing him with the support such that he does not need to go use the restroom inside the house. He gets taken out every 15, 20, or 30 minutes. Therefore he should not have a need to use the restroom inside of the house the rest of the time.

B. Don't even let it happen - When he does use the restroom inside the house, I dragged him out (too big of a pup to be picked up and carried) immediately, and yes with urine dripping on the floor from where he is all the way out to the doorway, to show him where the urine is supposed to go - outside the house. This sends him the message "no, it does not happen here".

With the combination of A) "support" and B) "don't even let it happen", you are on one side supporting him and meeting his needs such that he does not need to use restroom in the house, and on the other side you are giving him the message that we do not use the restroom inside of the house.

Coming back to our child. The A) "support" here for our child needs to be all of the things that I have talked about in the preceding meeting internal needs chapters in Section III, including having social stories to teach them, having token systems to support and reinforce the desirable behaviors, having regular routines and schedules to give them structure, having visual charts to help them make abstract things tangible and concrete, meeting their sensory needs, having transition strategies to set them up for success and giving them the tools to handle a transition. All of the above are your A) - support for the child such that undesirable behavior does not need to happen. In this chapter, I want to give you some specific examples on B) "don't even let it happen". In the case of dog training you are pulling the dog out while he has an undesirable behavior. You are pulling him out in that exact instant so he knows that it does not go there and it does not happen there.

Another example is from my own child. I have skipped a numerous amount of family meals to sit out in the parking lot at one hundred plus degrees in the middle of Texas. Why? Because I "don't even let it happen!" There was a period in our lives that one of our sons would whine, yell, scream, and have tantrums every time we ate at a restaurant. Of course, this was after we had done everything in A) "support" (sensory support was big for this son), and when it came to B), when that difficult behavior hit, my strategy was "don't even let it happen!" For example, (again, this is in addition to all of the supporting activities that I suggested), when we were in a restaurant, every time he would start whining or having problems I would immediately pick him up and take him out of the restaurant and he would not be allowed to go back in again. I would spend the entire family meal outing sitting in the heated Texas parking lot because I would put him in the van, walk out of his sight and supervise him, watching for his safety from a small distance where he could not see me and did not know that I was there. (Note: I would have been reinforcing and increasing his bad behavior if I was giving him my one-on-one attention as a result of his bad behavior). My message there is "no, we do not yell, scream, or whine in a restaurant (actually, you not do that anywhere)." My son quickly learned not to do that. He quickly learned exactly what was expected and what was not allowed in a restaurant.

The idea is that you fuel the desirable behaviors with success paradigm and success strategies, at the same time nipping in the bud the undesirable behaviors without giving undue attention. When I say undue attention I mean that as I'm pulling my child out of the restaurant I am not turning that into a one-on-one attention time for him.

How Far are You Willing to Go?

"Don't even let it happen" is much easier said than done. The reality is, for many of the undesirable behaviors, it takes a very large amount of effort to really not let it happen. In my restaurant example, are you willing to opt out of numerous family meal outings to sit out in one hundred plus degree heat just to make a point to your child? That is a big sacrifice you have to be willing to make. I was starving all of those times because I never ate as a result. There are many parents that either don't get it or are not willing to do that (but if you are reading this book, you get it and you are willing to go as far as you need to). I'm sure in your everyday life you have witnessed numerous situations in a grocery store or in the restaurant where a child is misbehaving and you hear the parent correcting, "no, do not do that", "No, I told you to stop that." But the behavior continues – that is, the parents continue to let it happen.

"But I just spent the last hour in the grocery store collecting my shopping cart full of groceries and I cannot walk out of there." This is what I'm talking about - the price sometimes is not cheap. I have walked out of grocery stores ditching a cart full of much needed groceries, for a family of 7 that I have spent the last hour collecting, just to make a point to my child about his misbehavior. So we wasted a whole trip and we had no groceries. (Mind you, getting 5 kids 5 and under ready for a grocery trip, buckling 5x3=15 buckles to get in the van, then unbuckling another 15 buckles to get out of the van, etc. is no walk in the park!) But what's not allowed is not allowed, and my actions have to say so.

How far am I willing to go? I have pulled a kicking and screaming misbehaving child of mine out of a store, across the street, through the parking lot and into the car while carrying a set of twin toddlers (one in each arm), holding the hand of a 4 year old, and an unborn infant in my belly. I don't even know how I made it to the car without losing a child. Was it a scene? Yes. Were people staring at me and my clan? Yes, the whole way out the store and to the car. Did I care? No. I carried an additional 80 lbs. of little people weight on me and I was 7 months pregnant. I needed to do what I needed to do.

And what was the result of my support along with numerous sacrifices? Because I have paid the price to make those important points come across to my children, I am now able to have relatively smooth shopping trips with all my children. I'll tell you it looks like a breeze from the outside. I get frequent comments from people in the stores or restaurants "your children are so well behaved." I get people getting out of their dining table to walk over to our table just to complement our children in absolute amusement. Boy, do they know the price I paid? Do they know all that goes in there? What they see is 5 young children all in order and well-behaved. They don't even know that I have some special needs children here in the mix who have the hardest time dealing with restaurants, shops, and situations outside of the house. They have no clue of all of the effort that I put into providing them support and avoiding the behavior altogether. But here I'm giving you the secret.

Another example, the well-known playground situation, where all the kids are on the playground playing and all the moms are standing or sitting on the side socializing away. There's nothing wrong with that picture except the fact that some of my kids, due to their Sensitive Divergent Needs and deficiencies, are not in a position to conduct themselves appropriately in the playground situation without specialized support. So I am there right next to my children the whole time creating little successes, giving numerous verbal acknowledgements of their good behaviors, sometimes even pulling them off to the side to show them a social story, giving them sensory breaks (yes even on the playground). And yes, standing right behind them ready to grab them off the playground should any inappropriate behaviors ever occur ("don't even let it happen!"). Many times I felt resentful of the fact that ALL the other moms got to just sit, relax and chat while I worked non-stop on the playground, but that's what was needed. Again, if you give them all the support they need, doing the things that I talked about in the previous chapters, then you will have a lot less need to take actions due to misbehaviors because you will be having fewer inappropriate behaviors.

More on Fueling

This chapter is for when all fails after you have given all the support you can. Even the best children raised by the best parents misbehave sometimes. Children are children and it is their job to test boundaries and experiment with what they can or cannot do. Your goal as a parent is to ensure that you provide sufficient, appropriate, and effective support for their success and for whatever behavior is "falling through the crack" you are going to nip it in the bud with your "don't even let it happen" strategy.

I cannot emphasize enough the importance of your fueling the desire to do right - having the child who feels like a success, a child who knows that they are awesome, a child who knows that your emotion is poured into their success, a child who knows that they have the power to choose any behavior they want yet have a strong desire to choose to do the right thing. Those things must be in place before you can come to this chapter and take a child out of the restaurant effectively.

The idea here is to fill the child's experience with success, to fill the child's whole life with success and your positive overpouring energy into their success, leaving no room at all in the child's life for misbehavior. Through your success building, misbehaviors will have no value in their lives. They will wake up every morning in ecstasy to have and feel more of that success (you want them to "feel high"). They will wake up every morning striving with a goal to triumph because triumph IS their history now. Misbehavior will no longer be a center of their lives; misbehaviors will become nothing but "accidents" in their lives.

Pay the Price

If you are still not convinced that you need to pay the price to not let certain behaviors happen, here is another way to put it - if you don't do what's hard now, you will pay for it big time later. You will pay for it later when it is established in your child's mind that it is okay to come and scream and yell in a restaurant during family meal outings and that the family and the restaurant will put up with it. In most cases if you can stop a behavior within the first few incidents when it first occurs, chances are highly likely that you will not see that behavior again in the future. So, pay the price now while it's still low (don't wait until your family stops having meals out altogether, per say).

The departing note of this chapter is to bring you back to the previous chapters relating to success - spend your energy on your children's success and <u>win them over with the taste of triumph</u> so that they will want more of it.

◆ ◆ ◆ ◆ ◆ ◆ ◆ ◆ ◆ ◆ ◆ ◆ ◆ ◆ ◆ ◆ ◆

Your Take-Away From This Chapter:

- ✓ Fuel your child's success (with success paradigm strategies)
- ✓ Support your child (with meeting the needs strategies)
- ✓ When it comes up unacceptable behaviors, be ridiculously firm with where you stand
- ✓ Be ready to pay the price

◆ ◆ ◆ ◆ ◆ ◆ ◆ ◆ ◆ ◆ ◆ ◆ ◆ ◆ ◆ ◆ ◆

CHAPTER 16
The Powerful Dialog That Beckons a Child's Inner Goodness

❖ ❖ ❖ ❖ ❖ ❖ ❖ ❖ ❖ ❖ ❖ ❖ ❖ ❖ ❖ ❖

What You Will Learn In This Chapter:

✓ Help your child identify his core being and bring out his goodness

❖ ❖ ❖ ❖ ❖ ❖ ❖ ❖ ❖ ❖ ❖ ❖ ❖ ❖ ❖ ❖

This chapter actually belongs to Section II – Success Paradigm, as the ideas behind this chapter have to do with placing your child in their success paradigm. However, I did not include this chapter there as I feel that it is important to have the "daily basics" (meeting the needs) implemented so that the daily support to meet the child's needs are in place before we get further into things that more behavioral in nature.

Once we address the child's needs, strategies in this chapter are more of a "chicken soup for the heart" nature. Over the years I have used some of these odd tricks to treat difficult behavior patterns. They are very effective and I want to share them with you here.

I think of them as "if all fails" tricks, but if you just want to use them before "all fail" that would be just fine.

"I want my Sam Back!"

This trick sounds very silly and it also can be very fun, but it is a trick that speaks to their most inner core identity – who they are. It is much deeper than the silly joke it sounds like. It reminds them of who they really are, how beautiful they are, and thus it is my favorite strategy. It brings out the best in them.

Again, rarely does one strategy alone work because these children really need lots of support in place, but if you have all the other pieces together from my other strategies, this would be a very nice and an extremely effective addition to your behavior toolbox.

There have been numerous times over the years when one of my children would get into a downward spiral with his misbehaviors, all very difficult behaviors, and most of them extremely dangerous to his own safety and the safety of others around him (his younger siblings). When he was on a roll, appearing to "live for" aggressive behaviors and knocking young siblings and infants down, I pulled him to a private corner and had a conversation with him – the "I want my ___ back" conversation. This is what that conversation looked like:

Me: (looking intensely into his eyes) "Where did my Sam (name of the child I'm speaking with) go?"

My child: "I'm right here!"

Me: "No, this is not my Sam! My Sam doesn't hit people; my Sam doesn't kick people; he doesn't hurt people. This is NOT my Sam. I want my Sam back!"

My child: "I AM Sam."

Me: "No, this person here is doing all kinds of hurtful things that my Sam doesn't do. He is wearing Sam's clothes and living inside Sam's skin, but he is not Sam. My Sam is kind; my Sam is thoughtful; my Sam is the one who helps his sister dress up like a princess and has tea parties with her; my Sam is the one who takes care of our baby and makes him laugh; my Sam cares about people; he is nothing but love. Give me my Sam back!"

My child: "But I AM here." (With big smiles because he finds this amusing)

Me: (smiling back and hugging my child) "Yeah! This IS my Sam! He is smiling; he is happy, kind, and full of love…. Sam, can you please just keep that unattractive creature out of here for me? I really didn't enjoy him, and I'm really glad that I got my Sam back now."

My child: (joyfully smiling) "Ok, I will smash him into pieces and flush him down the toilet, so he can't ever come back here again!"

Silly? It's actually a little deeper than it sounds. I'll explain momentarily.

Result? It worked like magic when immediately he changed his behaviors to ones that are more consistent with the wonderful being that he is. It works to snap them out of it (only if their needs are met though). And then, of course, you know that I'm going to say this again – support, support, support, and continue to be head-over-toes excited about their every little success. This is just to snap them out of it and ignite it so to speak; you still need to go back and do your job (provide support and fuel their desire to do right) ☺

It works for the young ones because not only do they find it amusing that you seem so confused, but you can just see their eyes sparkle at the idea of you thinking such high thoughts about them. (A more mature version of the same conversation works for the older ones too). It kicks them into seeing themselves in a different way – seeing themselves as the beautiful human being that they are. It snaps them out of the downward spiral mode of living to see what more stunningly terrible things they can accomplish that day. When you keep insisting that this little man in front of you is not your Sam and he knows he IS the Sam, he is forced to question his identity. Then with your concise description of all the good things Sam _does_, all the good qualities Sam _has_, and just the beautiful being that Sam _is_, he is forced to reunite with his core being as a magnificent creature. How powerful is it that someone finds himself as the most beautiful being and in turn overflows his beauty into every part of his actions. The most powerful behavior change you can have comes from within - the inner child knowing who he is. His action becomes only an artifact of who he is. This is the ultimate – a child who knows who he is and walks his own path, regardless of what's going on outside of him.

What if my child is older and this would just be far too silly to bring up? The idea that "YOU are beautiful and perfect the way you are" doesn't change. The same message is equally empowering; the idea is the same. But you can tailor your language to your child's needs. For example, I had this same conversation with my older son once when I matched his language as he was into Literary Analysis at the time. I told him that he is the "protagonist" who wants so badly to be loving, kind, and all the great things that he is. He is also the "heroine" who _IS_ loving, kind, and magnificent. But his "antagonist" is getting the better of him when he acts out. And again, "I want my Sam back!"

You must point out not only the good things your child _does_ (concrete actions), the good qualities your child _has_, but most importantly, the beautiful being that he _is_. The last part about what he is says "No matter what you do, you are still beautiful, awesome, and extremely valuable inside. No matter what actions you choose, it does not change who you are." And that's powerful because upon a call to reunite with his inner self, he doesn't have to feel ashamed of himself for all the awful things he has done, but rather, he is liberated to appreciate himself as an amazing being.

Preemptive Praise

"You are sitting so calmly and so controlled. You are exerting far more inner power of self-control and discipline for yourself. I am so proud of your level of self-control!"

The trick is to give a preemptive praise like this to your child when you know he is about to go down the wrong path. It puts a pause on his impulse behavior and gives him a chance to insert a logical thought before he acts irrationally. And the logical thought you are inserting here is, "I've been contemplating on kicking him, but I didn't, because I'm above that. I'm better than that." Once you have a child who thinks he is great and feels he is great, his actions will be aligned with his feelings and beliefs about himself. You are helping them empower themselves. This strategy is rooted in that new paradigm – "I'm a success!"

In that moment, even though the real truth is that your child is just about to kick that other boy, you do not want to say what's typically heard -- "Don't you even think about it!" "Don't kick him". You don't want your child to feel that your assumptions of him are negative. Instead, you want to give your child credit and appreciation for "having not kicked him yet", which is, in itself, is a success. By doing so, you are then giving him one success to ride on – "I haven't kicked him even though I really wanted to, so I'm being successful. Because I'm bigger than this, I can actually just walk away from this situation altogether." Now you have just defused a would-have-gone-wrong situation using the child's own sense of high self-esteem.

Assume They Have Good Intentions
Even in a bad moment, it is crucial that you assume their intentions are good. No child wakes up in the morning thinking that they want to do the absolute most terrible thing they can do today.

If you know with certainty that their intention behind a specific poor behavior was ill-natured, then you need to use the "I want my Sam back" strategy to reconnect your child to their inner beauty. No human is born to be devious and destructive. Behind every poor behavior, even in the extreme case of murder from an adult, there is beauty in their inner core being and there are disconnects, hurts, and fears or what not that drove the poor conduct.

Unless you know for a fact that the intention behind a specific poor behavior was ill-natured (in which case you use "I want my Sam back" strategy), you need to assume they have good intentions. Some behaviors call for a discussion while others don't (a natural consequence is all that it needs). You can be the judge. For behaviors that you actually want to talk about, you first assume their good intention in your chat and I will show you how. Before we talk about what that conversation should look like, please note that there is a good time and a bad time to speak with your child about a specific poor behavior. Please refer to the chapter: Behavior ABC to understand when is a good time to talk with your child about a behavior problem. Talking about a behavior problem with your child at the wrong time can dramatically increase the problem behavior.

When you talk to your child about a specific poor behavior, let them know:

1. You understand their needs and you understand that their intentions are good,
2. The negative impact of their chosen behavior, and
3. Behaviors that can live out their good intentions more effectively

For example,

> "Benny, you really wanted to be the helper today. You wanted to help everybody get their smoothie cups, and you wanted to help everyone so much that you ran over Chris and Kelly to make sure you get to the cups before they did. You just wanted to help them, didn't you? Well, when you ran over them to do so, they fell down and got hurt, and they also felt bad for not being able to choose their own cups. What do you think you could do next time so they know that you care for them and you want to help them?" (Then come up with better solutions together)

The story is how you frame it. In this case, there was a bit of a controlling and competitive nature that Benny wanted to have control over what cups other people got, and he also wanted to be the first to bring the cups for them. But you omit the rest and stick with the part that is well intentioned. When you frame it this way, they are not so defensive. They are able to better open up to options of doing it better next time. It also shows them that you understand where they are coming from – that they can put their defenses down and work together with you on this. You may have some other incidences when 100% of it was well intentioned. Either way it is important to give them the benefit of the doubt and assume the best.

◆ ◆ ◆ ◆ ◆ ◆ ◆ ◆ ◆ ◆ ◆ ◆ ◆ ◆ ◆ ◆

Your Take-Away From This Chapter:

- ✓ "I want my Sam back":
  - o Remind your child the beautiful being that he is - his identify.
  - o When he is reconnected with his magnificent core, he will once again be that beautiful being.
- ✓ Preemptive praise:
  - o Catch your child when you know a misbehavior is most likely coming, give him credit and appreciate him for having NOT misbehaved.
  - o Your appreciation will be his drive to make the right choice in that moment.
- ✓ Assume they have good intentions

◆ ◆ ◆ ◆ ◆ ◆ ◆ ◆ ◆ ◆ ◆ ◆ ◆ ◆ ◆ ◆

CHAPTER 17
Encouragement

Caring for a child with SDN can be a very challenging and discouraging task. The journey will have you doubting yourself - Am I doing the right thing? Am I a good parent/teacher/caregiver? But if you are reading this book, you are a good parent, teacher, professional, or caregiver.

If you are a parent and you ever get the judgmental eyes while you're out with your child with SDN in public, be empowered to say "He is a great child, and I'm a great parent. Walk a mile in my shoes and you'll see what a fantastic job I'm already doing!"

Besides the child, I want to empower you as a caregiver to live beyond judgements and natural or societal limitations. You can only take your child beyond the limits of his conditions, *from outcast to outstanding*, when you can live above these limitations yourself.

Apply these strategies with your child, be consistent, and don't give up. Remember the Theater Child who was the King Arthur and believed he could be anything? After applying the strategies in this book, he is well on his way *from outcast to outstanding*. The King Arthur figure in the Harmonious Clan logo represents the Theater Child, and he is there as a reminder to you: Keep the **zestfulness in YOUR King Arthur**, who believes he is undefeatable, and he can be anything he wants.

AFTERWORD: TAKING THE FIRST STEP

The concepts I detailed here took me years to discover based on a lot of research, work with professionals and tons of trial and error. I wish I had something like this when I first started.

Right now, you may feel overwhelmed from the amount of information in this book, but I hope you'll realize that this actually is a shortcut. What is the alternative? Continuing to stretch yourself beyond your physical and emotional energy, time, and capacity, trying to get results; but instead getting only frustration? That path will take its toll on both you and your child.

The sooner you polish off the rough surface and get to the diamond, the sooner you get to enjoy your child. Now you have a choice to make– you can either follow the short cut in this book where things are laid out step by step for you, where you can gain from my struggle, or you can take the alternate path. On the alternative path, you will encounter the struggles I already went through. You will get there, but why not save time and frustration and use the strategies I discuss in this book? Even though not all the concepts will apply to you or your child, you will find many useful tools that you can employ. I went through years of research, working with professionals, trials and errors, tears and pain, and I put this information together here for you so that you don't have to pay the price I paid.

You now have the information that cuts to the chase and _saves you the time, physical and emotional energy, and money spent trying to figure this all out on your own while your child_ *is growing up.* **You have a stepping stone to take and tweak into something that works specifically for your situation instead of starting from scratch.**

Your child is growing and time is going by. Do you really want to spend many years to get to a great place? The time you lose will never come back. Or do you just want to take these proven strategies and shorten your learning curve? You want to have the result right now, so you can enjoy your child and your child can be on the path to outstanding.

I have assisted a multitude of children/students and parents in taking that first step on the path to outstanding. I would love to do the same with you. If you'd like to work more closely with me, I invite you to a free One on One consult. We can work together to help you learn how to bridge the gap between where you are to where you want to be with your child, your parenting life, your family, your own life and the future of your child.

To take the first step, simply book for a free One on One consult at www.harmoniousclan.com/one-on-one/.

I also have many resources on our website to help you learn more, including educational podcasts, downloadable resources, and e-books.

I want to help you stop wasting time being frustrated with your child or your situation, start enjoying timeless memories with your child and revealing your precious gem. Remember, inside the outer rough surface is the fine gemstone that is your real child. Once polished, all of your child's talents, genius, and beauty will finally shine through.

Confucius said,

> "I hear and I forget.
> I see and I remember.
> I do and I understand."

Let's do it together!

Luiza Coscia

APPENDIX: SELECTING THE RIGHT PROFESSIONALS

◆ ◆ ◆ ◆ ◆ ◆ ◆ ◆ ◆ ◆ ◆ ◆ ◆ ◆ ◆ ◆ ◆

What You Will Learn In This Appendix:

- ✓ The types professionals to consult with should your child have the need
- ✓ Description of what each profession does
- ✓ The most effective ways to partner with a professions

◆ ◆ ◆ ◆ ◆ ◆ ◆ ◆ ◆ ◆ ◆ ◆ ◆ ◆ ◆ ◆ ◆

Caveat for This Appendix:

This appendix is not meant to overwhelm you or urge you to put another item (such as seek professionals) on your to-do list, because not every child with SDN and family needs it. This appendix is meant to be a resource only IF you feel that you need to take your child to a professional, so no need to feel like you HAVE TO go make an appointment.

The value of this book is that it is a synthesis of accumulated multi-disciplinary professional advice (through numerous face-to-face meetings and books) combined with our tested and proven real life experimentation with our children. It is designed to guide parents and caregivers of Children with SDN through the information overload to proven practical strategies that you can implement today. This appendix is meant as a resource if you need it.

Where do the Strategies in This Book and Professionals Come Together?

The strategies in this book are powerful and they work, but they do not replace any medical or professional services that your child may need; the strategies are meant to complement any necessary medical and professional care. Some children are already in every doctor and professional's offices and still struggling with day-to-day life, school, homework, routines, and behaviors and that's when the strategies in this book come into play. The doctors, therapists, and professionals don't live in your child's house and aren't day-to-day caregivers of your child - your child needs more on a day-to-day and consistent basis in between these appointments. My suggestion is: in conjunction with any necessary medical and professional care your child is receiving, apply the strategies in this book in your child's everyday life to complement the care and create well-rounded support for your child from all angles. Home life and school life are a bulk of a child's life hours. These hours are so important in shaping your child's development and helping him achieve all that he is born and meant to achieve. This book is written to help your child do so.

As discussed, a child with SDN can have any or none of these conditions: ADHD, Autism, Sensory Processing Disorder, Bipolar, Gifted, Twice Exceptional (2E); Anxiety Disorder, Oppositional Defiance Disorder, etc. Sometimes meeting your child's needs means working with one or a few medical professionals in conjunction with implementing the strategies in this book at home and school; other times, just the strategies in this book alone are enough to meet your child's needs. If your child needs any medical or professional care, below are some tips on selecting good providers and partnering effectively with them.

Psychiatrist

I personally subscribe to a natural approach to everything. I will try everything I can to NOT medicate a child, but in many instances, mediation is needed to help a child level things out and get a grip on things. It can help take the edge off so things are more manageable. If that is the case, here is my advice on partnering with a psychiatrist:

1) Work closely with your psychiatrist to find just the right "cocktail of drugs" that levels things out for your child. Sometimes it's one medication, sometimes it's a mix of drugs. Upon every new medication, take careful notes and journals about your child's response and report your notes back to your psychiatrist so that he/she can help tweak the drug type and dosage to find just the right "cocktail of drugs". A good psychiatrist listens carefully, works closely with you, and is willing to adjust medications and dosages in between appointments based on patient's response to medication. The psychiatrist should generally work with you to get the 'right' effective dosage for your child, so that it is just the right dosage to help your child while minimizing side effects. You want to strive for the minimum effective dose to get the indicated results and avoid over medicating your child.
2) Do not rely solely on medication. In the case of depression, anxiety and various other conditions, if your child

is on medication, it will help take the edge off, but it is most helpful if you are working with other professionals or at home on the underlying issues. For example, in the case of Autism, Bipolar and/or ADHD symptoms, the medication helps level things out for a child such that he is in better condition to receive training on needed life skills such as self-regulation, impulse control, focus and attention, calming techniques, coping skills, etc. Use medications (in my opinion, only if necessary) to bring your child to a more manageable and receptive state to learn the life skills needed. Ultimately, your child still needs to obtain certain life skills to conquer his challenges in life.

Psychologist

A psychologist can diagnose and help you resolve matters having to do with emotional and behavioral problems. They can evaluate children for various disorders such as anxiety, depression, attention deficit disorder, etc. A psychologist can use Cognitive Behavioral Therapy and other techniques to help children obtain coping skills, other important life skills, and good mental health.

Developmental Pediatrician (MD)

A developmental Pediatrician can diagnose various developmental delays or disabilities including Autism, ADHD, and various learning disabilities. They usually spend a good amount of time evaluating the child for any abnormalities in the areas of development and learning. This includes developmental problems related to prematurity. They can also prescribe medication when necessary. A good developmental pediatrician will serve as not only a medical professional for evaluation, diagnosis and medication management, but will also serve as an advocate for your child to ensure that your child receives any qualified services through the school or state early intervention programs. A good developmental pediatrician can also guide you through the process of care coordination and provide direction should your child need care from multiple areas such as Occupational Therapy and Speech Therapy, etc.

Occupational Therapist

Occupational Therapists are commonly known to help with gross and fine motor skills or functions such as feeding for children with difficulties. An Occupational Therapist can also assess your child for any sensory integration issues and help your child address the dysfunctions, so that your child can achieve better sensory integration. When you work with an occupational therapist, he/she may work on a number of exercises during each session. My advice is to try your best to have your child do some of those exercises at home. Only once a week of working on those items with a therapist isn't as effective as doing them more frequently and integrating them into part of your child's daily life.

Speech Therapist (Speech Language Pathologist)

A speech therapist can help your child with any speech related problems including articulation, expressive and receptive language delays, social language use or pragmatic disorders, fluency, auditory processing disorder, language disorder, etc. They can even help with oral motor and oral feeding difficulties. If your child struggles with any of the above, have your child evaluated by a Speech Language Pathologist. They can make recommendations and also carry on the treatment plan. Speech Therapy is most effective with high parent involvement. At home, outside of therapy time, try to practice whatever your child worked on during therapy time so that your child can get the most out of it.

Behavior Therapist (Board Certified Behavior Analyst, BCBA)

While I shared many behavioral strategies in this book, if you need to go deeper in this area, a Board Certified Behavioral Analyst would be the right person to consult or work with. They analyze various aspects of behaviors, and create a plan to modify the undesirable behaviors and replace them with more appropriate behaviors. A BCBA typically performs behavioral analysis, designs a comprehensive intervention plan, and then supervises Registered Behavior Technicians and other behavior therapists who implement the intervention plan. This sometimes can require a large number of therapy hours per week depending on the child and the challenges.

Developmental or Behavioral Optometrist

Vision is more than seeing things clearly. It involves processing and making sense of what one sees. Some Children with SDN may experience difficulties with vision processing. If your child is struggling with reading or learning, consider an evaluation with a

Developmental or Behavioral Optometrist for potential vision processing problems. They can perform vision therapy to improve it. A regular Optometrist is to Developmental or Behavioral Optometrist what computer "hardware" is to "software". One cares for the physical "hardware" (structure and mechanics) of whether and how well the eyes can see, while the other cares for whether and how well one can process what the eyes see.

Audiologist

An audiologist can also assess how we process what we hear. If your child has auditory processing difficulties, you can consult with a Speech Language Pathologist for effected language processing issues as well as an audiologist for the auditory processing piece.

◆ ◆ ◆ ◆ ◆ ◆ ◆ ◆ ◆ ◆ ◆ ◆ ◆ ◆ ◆ ◆ ◆

Your Take-Away From This Appendix:

- ✓ If seeking the help of a professional is necessary for your child, take the time to find the right professional whom you trust
- ✓ Have a trusting partner relationship with these professionals while complementing their care with day-to-day strategies you are learning in this book

◆ ◆ ◆ ◆ ◆ ◆ ◆ ◆ ◆ ◆ ◆ ◆ ◆ ◆ ◆ ◆ ◆

SIX WAYS TO PUT OUTCAST TO OUTSTANDING TO WORK FOR YOU

1. **Visit Harmonious Clan website**
   www.harmoniousclan.com

2. **Ask for a free 'One on One Consult' where we can discuss your biggest concern**
   Go to: www.harmoniousclan.com/one-on-one to book a time

3. **Tell me your biggest struggle & I'll provide you with a personal response**
   www.harmoniousclan.com/need-help/

4. **Download our free e-book: 5 Little Wins that are proven to improve your child's behavior in just 13 minutes a day!**
   www.harmoniousclan.com/books/5-little-wins-ebook/

5. **Listen to our educational podcasts**
   www.harmoniousclan.com/podcast-episodes/
   You can also listen to our podcasts on iTunes, Stitcher, Google Play

6. **Register for a Harmonious Clan course**
   www.harmoniousclan.com/courses/

7. **Send me an email with questions or comments**
   luiza@harmoniousclan.com

Harmonious Clan is all about equipping you with proven practical strategies we've developed over the years through our own experiences and trials and errors, filtering out the noise and synthesizing what works, bringing you strategies that give you results, **enabling you to nurture your child from outcast to outstanding**. We do this by resourcing you with our books, educational podcasts, courses, a supportive community, speaking events and one on one consulting.

ABOUT THE AUTHOR

Luiza Y. Coscia has a Bachelor's of Science degree in engineering and earned her real life PhD in child behavior while raising and homeschooling her 5 children who required creative interventions due to special needs. During a successful engineering career, Luiza honed her problem solving and analytical skills, skills that she now uniquely applies to child behavior in order to nurture the diamond in the rough. Just as she developed tutoring methods that brought a multitude of struggling students from C to A while in college, she uses similar methods to develop strategies that effectively address the actual underlying cause of behaviors, and achieves behavioral transformations by not simply treating the symptoms. Her personable, friendly approach and real-life perspective is what sets her and this book apart.

Contact Luiza:

If you have questions, comments, or need additional information or support, please email me at luiza@harmoniousclan.com and visit us at www.harmoniousclan.com, where our mission is: **Enabling you to nurture your child from outcast to outstanding.**

www.ingramcontent.com/pod-product-compliance
Lightning Source LLC
Chambersburg PA
CBHW020836160426
43192CB00007B/679